PLATT NATIONAL PARK

PLATT NATIONAL PARK

ENVIRONMENT AND ECOLOGY

BY BALLARD M. BARKER
AND WILLIAM CARL JAMESON

University of Oklahoma Press : Norman

Library of Congress Cataloging in Publication Data

Barker, Ballard M.
    Platt National Park : environment and ecology.

    Bibliography: p.
    1. Platt National Park. I. Jameson, William Carl,
joint author. II. Title.
F702.P7B37   917.66'57   74–15909
ISBN 0–8061–1256–5

PREFACE

For years national parks have offered the public something which seems to be necessary to all human beings, be they young or old, male or female, scientist or student. Whatever this basic human requirement is—whether it takes the form of recreation or merely the need to be outdoors—Americans look to their national parks for its fulfillment. It is apparent that more and more of us are aware of this need, for as pollution and the pressures of urban living are rapidly increasing, so are the visitation rates at the national parks.

This book is designed to serve as an introduction to many of the natural and cultural aspects of Platt National Park. It is intended to familiarize the reader with the diverse environments he will encounter while traveling through the park. Perhaps more significant, it is intended to create an awareness of the delicate yet vital ecological relationships which not only are apparent in the park but exist in one form or another throughout the entire world.

This guide is intended to go beyond the traditional field guide. We feel that understanding environmental relationships is far more important than merely identifying separate components of a natural community. With this in mind, the reader will come to understand some basic and underlying ecological assumptions, and we trust that, through an understanding and appreciation of these concepts, the total environmental picture of the world we live in will be more fully realized and admired for what it is. In addition, it is hoped the reader will have a greater appreciation of the role each and every person has in this dynamic system.

This book is the result of the combined efforts of several persons. The original idea, as well as many supportive ideas and contributions, must be shared with our associates in the Department of Geography of the University of Oklahoma.

Joseph B. Schiel, Jr., must be credited for the initial proposal of preparing this manuscript, and it was largely under his direction that much of the research in the park was conducted. John D. Gunter deserves special credit for his interpretation of the geological history of the area. Others who provided substantive contributions were James B. Humphries, Jr., and Charles E. Webb. Chester Weems was responsible for most of the photographs appearing in this book. Many thanks are due the naturalists at the Platt National Park Travertine Nature Center, who gave freely of their time to aid us in the preparation of materials. Special gratitude is felt for John W. Morris, who was responsible for the preliminary editing of the manuscript. Without his help and encouragement this book would not have been possible.

Lastly there is the debt owed our wives, Carol and Molly, who typed the manuscript and tolerated the whole endeavor.

West Point, New York   Ballard M. Barker
Norman, Oklahoma   William Carl Jameson
July 31, 1974

CONTENTS

ILLUSTRATIONS

PHOTOGRAPHS

FIGURES

PLATT NATIONAL PARK

1

INTRODUCTION TO THE PARK

Platt National Park is situated in south central Oklahoma at the juncture of the southern Osage Plains and the ancient, worn remnants of the Arbuckle Mountains. Lying as it does nearly midway between Oklahoma City, Oklahoma, and Dallas, Texas, in a portion of the United States which many persons stereotype as mile after mile of rather drab and unspectacular subprairie scenery, Platt National Park each year attracts more visitors than two-thirds of all other national parks. These visitors, many of whom return year after year, come to this smallest of all national parks (only 912 acres, about one and one-half square miles) for the same reasons that both man and beast have come for centuries. They come to enjoy the cool and tranquil beauty of the simple wooded valley and its many springs and streams. In the past the fresh-water springs formed a dependable prairie oasis that supplied all comers, and the mineral-water springs very early gained for the site a reputation as one of America's leading health spas. In addition to those who visit the park

3

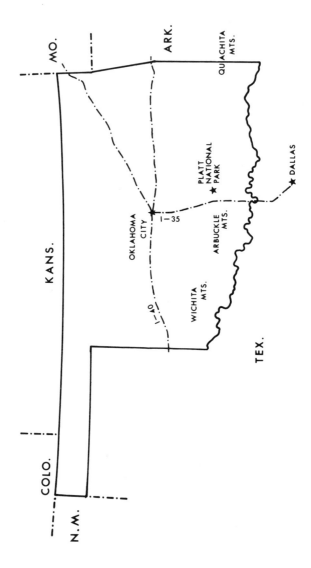

Sulphur entrance to Platt National Park. Photo by Chester Weems.

primarily for rest and relaxation, recent years have seen an increase in the number of visitors who come to participate in a wide range of environmental and nature programs which are conducted by the naturalists of the park's Travertine Nature Center.

The area of the park effectively encompasses three miles of the beautifully wooded valleys of Rock and Travertine creeks, several hundred acres of upland prairie, and, most significantly, more than thirty springs is-

Figure 1 (opposite). Platt National Park, the nation's smallest national park, is situated in south-central Oklahoma, about midway between Oklahoma City, Oklahoma, and Dallas, Texas.

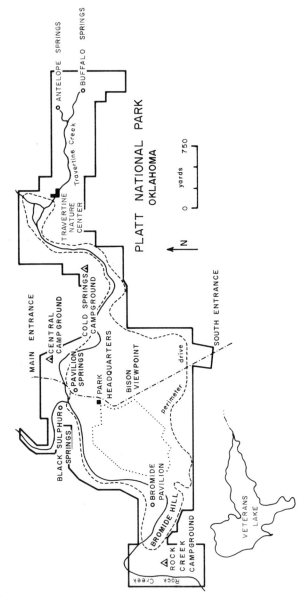

PLATT NATIONAL PARK
OKLAHOMA

N

0   750
yards

ANTELOPE SPRINGS
BUFFALO SPRINGS
Travertine Creek
TRAVERTINE NATURE CENTER
COLD SPRINGS CAMPGROUND
CENTRAL CAMPGROUND
MAIN ENTRANCE
PAVILION SPRINGS
PARK HEADQUARTERS
BISON VIEWPOINT
perimeter drive
SOUTH ENTRANCE
BLACK SULPHUR SPRINGS
BROMIDE PAVILION
BROMIDE HILL
ROCK CREEK CAMPGROUND
Rock Creek
VETERANS LAKE

6

suing either fresh or mineral water. Perhaps the unique and most interesting aspect of the park, especially for persons interested in ecology or plant geography, is that within a small area are many observable and conveniently accessible phases of a major ecotone.[1] It is an area where eastern broadleaf forest and western steppe-type grassland occur adjacent to each other in a region which has a climatic pattern not considered optimal for either. The variations in the vegetation types and their associated natural communities occur both horizontally and vertically on the landscape. Each of these natural zones contain a series of different micro-habitats and are the result of the complex interrelationships of soil and bedrock, living organisms, surface and ground water, and atmosphere.

PARK ATTRACTIONS AND FACILITIES

Fresh Water Springs
The park's waters have always been one of the area's greatest attractions, and many years ago the local Indians named it Peaceful Valley of Rippling Waters. Much of the water in the park comes from Buffalo Springs and Antelope Springs in the eastern end of the park, which

[1]*An ecotone is an area in transition between two or more natural communities. In Platt National Park it is represented by the meeting of forest and grassland communities.*

Figure 2 (opposite). Platt National Park.

7

Antelope Springs. Photo by Chester Weems.

flow about five million gallons of water a day during normal years. They are most interesting because of their beauty and size, and for their role as the sole source of Travertine Creek. Buffalo Springs surfaces to form a rock-bound pool in a restful glade near the eastern end of the park. A few hundred feet northwest of Buffalo Springs is a ledge of conglomerate rock from which Antelope Springs issues in its natural setting to form one of the park's most pleasant retreats. Both springs are situated along the main foot trail that loops through the woodland of the eastern portion of the park.

Mineral Springs

There are numerous cold-water mineral springs in the park which give rise to sulphur, bromide, and iron-bearing waters. Most of them are enclosed in pavilions or pools constructed of native stone and shaded by groves of large, old trees which present a pleasant and comfortable setting for the use and enjoyment of the springs. The central portion of the park near the main entrance contains the most significant sulphur springs at Hillside Spring, Pavilion Spring, and Black Sulphur Spring. In addition, Flower Park contains pools of sulphur water and mud which historically had some therapeutic qualities attributed to it. The major bromide springs are Medicine Spring and Bromide Spring, both of which are located in the same pavilion in the western portion of the park and, appropriately enough, rise from the base of Bromide Hill.

Unlike Hot Springs National Park, in Arkansas, which in the past maintained facilities for various mineral-water therapies, Platt National Park has no publicly owned bathhouse. The National Park Service makes

The Pavilion of Bromide and Medicine springs. Photo by Chester Weems.

available and maintains the various springs for all visitors but, though indicating their mineral composition, makes no claims about their medicinal or therapeutic values.

Travertine and Rock Creeks

Travertine Creek is the focus of Platt National Park from its source at Buffalo and Antelope springs to its juncture with Rock Creek near the center of the park. Since its only source of water is the springs, periods of prolonged drought which dry the springs also result in an absence of stream flow. Such occurrences are infrequent and temporary, however, and most of the time the stream

One of the many popular wading pools along Travertine Creek.

enhances the natural setting of the forest east of the Nature Center and provides many fine picnic sites and wading pools along the remainder of its course. A unique feature of this stream is its ability to form an unusual rock called travertine, from which the stream gets its name. The water of the stream is so highly charged with dissolved calcium carbonate that upon exposure to the atmosphere much of the mineral will precipitate to form a buff-colored deposit. Large accumulations form a porous travertine rock. Plant leaves and branches along the stream may be covered with a film of travertine dust that is precipitated from wind-blown spray.

Rock Creek is a large year-round stream which enters

Two of the park's resident bison at the Bison Viewpoint. Photo by Chester Weems.

Platt from the city of Sulphur and flows westward through the remainder of the park. Because of its size and permanence, this stream provides the additional opportunity for fishing, for which no license is required within the park boundaries.

Bromide Hill

This nearly vertical wooded bluff rises 140 feet above its base at Bromide Spring and Rock Creek. Along its top is found one of the most obvious ecotones in the area, where a growth of dense oak, ash, and elm vanishes and short grass and prickly-pear cactus become predominant. One can see for several miles in all directions from the Bromide Overlook, a vantage point from which the various natural landscapes of the park can be seen from a different perspective, as well as the Arbuckle Mountains and the Washita River valley on the southwest. In years gone by this hill was called Robbers' Roost because early-day outlaws used it as a lookout point.

The Bison Range
A portion of the park's upland prairie has been reserved as a range for a small herd of American Bison, more commonly known as buffalo. Although the springs of the park were once a favorite watering hole of large herds of bison which roamed this area, increased settlement led to the elimination of the animal in the last half of the nineteenth century. The small herd present in the park today is descended from a group of six bison which were obtained from the Wichita National Wildlife Refuge in western Oklahoma and Yellowstone National Park in 1920. These prairie giants are most often and easily seen in the afternoon from the main Bison Viewpoint on Highway 177, just south of the park headquarters.

Travertine Nature Center
The Travertine Nature Center is built across Travertine Creek in the eastern end of the park and is the focal point for most of the park's educational and interpretive activities. When it was established in 1969, it was only the second center of its kind in the national-park system. Its purpose is to provide a center for conducting nature and environmental study programs for both casual park visitors and the school children, college students, and adults of the surrounding region. The naturalists who conduct the activities at the Nature Center hope to cre-

The Travertine Nature Center and Gateway to the Environmental Study Area. Photo by Chester Weems.

ate or renew in the visitor an appreciation of the importance and beauty of even the simplest interrelationships in nature.

The Nature Center contains many exhibits of plants and animals in their natural settings. In addition there are a demonstration room, a library, workrooms, an information desk, a sales desk for books and cards, and an auditorium for the visitor's use. The auditorium is used for a full schedule of slide shows and motion pictures on a wide range of subjects dealing with conservation, the outdoors, and natural science. Many of the nature walks—guided and narrated by naturalists—also depart from the Nature Center. For maximum enjoyment and

A self-guiding nature trail in the Environmental Study Area. Photo by Chester Weems.

understanding, a tour of the park should begin with a visit to the Travertine Nature Center.

Environmental Study Area
The park area along Travertine Creek east of the Travertine Nature Center has been reserved as an Environmental Study Area, and as such is the outdoor classroom for many of the Nature Center's interpretative activities. It is designed to present the park visitor with a segment of the landscape which has minimal human disruption. The only access to this area is by foot trail, and its real value is appreciated only by the person who takes the time to sit quietly along a portion of the stream or trail and let

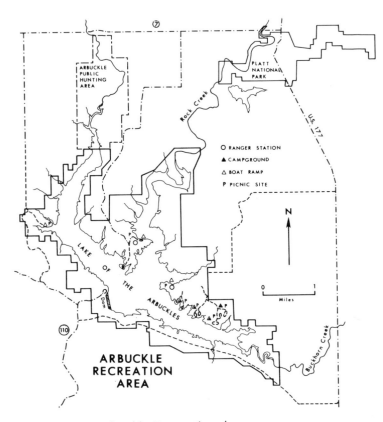

Figure 3. Arbuckle Recreation Area.

nature come to him. Naturalists from the Travertine Nature Center make scheduled guided walks through this area.

Perimeter Drive

For the visitor who has limited time or who first wishes

to get an over-all look at the park before settling down to a detailed visit, the six-mile perimeter drive is a worthwhile experience. This leisurely automobile drive starts at the Travertine Nature Center and takes the visitor to many of the points of interest and beauty while generally following the park boundary. An excellent guide pamphlet is provided free of charge at the Nature Center.

Picnicking and Camping
The park contains many picnic areas, all of which are completely equipped and situated in very attractive and pleasant areas. There are also over two hundred well-equipped and modern campsites in Central, Cold Springs, and Rock Creek campgrounds.

Arbuckle Recreation Area
Although not an integral part of Platt National Park, the Arbuckle Recreation Area, eight miles southwest, is under the administrative control of Platt National Park and offers an extension of the park's recreational opportunities. The area includes a twenty-four-hundred-acre artificial lake of deep, clear water which is impounded between forested and rocky ridges of the Arbuckle Mountains. The lake was formed in 1962 by the construction of a large rock and earth dam near the confluence of Platt National Park's Rock Creek and the Buckhorn and Guy Sandy creeks. Fishing, swimming, water-skiing, and skin diving are permitted at the lake. The land around the lake's shoreline is also included in the recreation area and maintains facilities for picnicking, camping, and boating. Much of the area is also reserved as a public hunting and trapping area.

CULTURAL HISTORY OF THE PARK

Early Occupancy

The first visitors to the area now included in Platt National Park were undoubtedly some of the southern Plains Indian tribes who lived and traveled in this region during prehistoric times. Those tribes included the Osages on the north and the Caddoes, Wichitas, Kiowas, and Comanches farther west near the Wichita Mountains. The earliest European influence and sovereignty in the region was alternately exercised by the Spaniards and the French until 1803, when the entire area was included in the Louisiana Purchase. The effects of those early contacts were negligible, however, and the United States government perpetuated the relative isolation of the area by generally excluding it from white settlement for several more decades.

Probably the first white men to travel through the area of the park were United States cavalrymen from Fort Smith, Arkansas, who patroled the area north of the Texas border in 1819 to expel illegal white settlers. Fort Gibson and Fort Towson were established in eastern Oklahoma in 1824 and assumed sole responsibility for frontier police action until 1842, when Fort Washita was built several miles south of the park's present location. In 1852, Fort Arbuckle was established just west of the park near the present town of Davis. It and Fort Washita had the mission of protecting the peaceful Choctaws and Chickasaws from the more warlike bands roaming

Figure 4 (opposite). The boundaries of Indian nations and the locations of prominent army posts during the early 1860's.

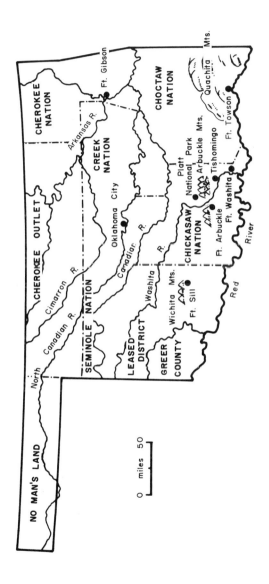

the area. Troops from these posts also did minor exploration and assisted parties of westward-bound emigrants. Both Fort Arbuckle and Fort Washita were abandoned in 1870, when Fort Sill was established near the Wichita Mountains of western Oklahoma.

The first permanent settlers in the park area were, strangely enough, neither local Indians nor white men but members of two woodland Indian tribes from the southeastern United States. In 1820 the United States government bowed to political and economic pressures in the Southeast and decided to remove all native Indian tribes from their lands east of the Mississippi River. Primarily affected by this decision were the Five Civilized Tribes, which were the most peaceful, prosperous, and advanced Indians in North America. Beginning in that year, representatives of the harassed Cherokees, Choctaws, Creeks, Chickasaws, and Seminoles were constrained to sign a series of treaties with the United States which would remove them forever from their traditional homes in North Carolina, Tennessee, Georgia, Alabama, Florida, and Mississippi. They were to surrender tribal lands east of the Mississippi River in return for perpetual, unmolested, and self-governed territory in Arkansas and Oklahoma. Reluctantly, the Choctaws, Chickasaws, and Cherokees migrated west between 1835 and 1847 under harsh and often tragic conditions; among the most notable of these Indian experiences was the infamous "Trail of Tears," which took place in 1838. The Choctaws and Chickasaws then settled on their assigned lands between the Texas border and the South Canadian River, just north of the present park site.

Once established in this new land, the Indians quickly resumed the same high level of civilization they had been forced to abandon in the East. Farms and cattle ranches were the basis of the economy, and the Indian councils established a system of public education, courts, police, and other functions of government considered appropriate anywhere in the United States in that era. In addition to normal commerce and administrative functions of the army and the Bureau of Indian Affairs, Indian lands around the park were increasingly frequented by cattle drives and emigrant trains until the closing of the frontier. The famous Chisholm Trail from Texas to Kansas passed between Fort Arbuckle and Fort Sill on the west, and the Texas or Shawnee Trail angled northwestward just fifty miles southeast of the park. Occasional longhorn and local cattle drives were made up the Washita River valley adjacent to the park's present location. A branch of the Marcy Trail used by some emigrants also passed through the area. In 1872 the Missouri, Kansas, and Texas Railway was completed across the Indian Territory along the general trace of the Texas Trail, and the late 1880's saw the construction of the north-to-south Santa Fe Railway from Guthrie through Davis and on to Texas.

During this period, as for all time before, the abundant and reliable springs of the valley of Travertine and Rock creeks provided a welcome oasis for the great herds of bison, antelope, and cattle which frequented the vicinity. Buffalo and Antelope springs were favorite watering holes for bison and antelope, as well as Indian cattle and horses. The heavy use of the springs reduced them to large trodden areas of muddy bog. Buffalo Springs alone covered nearly one-half acre and was called "Buffalo Suck" because of the bison's way of drinking water from shallow puddles and rivulets.

Establishment of the Park

By 1880 white ranchers had begun to move into the area to establish cattle ranches on land leased from the Chickasaw Nation or acquired through marriage to Indian women. Eventually that influx caused the Indians to lose all practical control of their tribal lands, and white political and economic interests spurred increasing demands for establishment of formal United States control of the area. As the Indian Territory moved closer to statehood, the Chickasaws and Choctaws became increasingly fearful that their traditional spring and summer camping ground along Rock Creek would be taken into private ownership and lost to them forever. In fact, the town of Sulphur was already growing up around the mineral springs. To prevent the possibility of losing their lands altogether, the tribes ceded the area of the park to the United States government in 1902 so that the springs could be used "by all men for perpetuity." Sulphur was eventually relocated on higher ground away from the springs, and the Sulphur Springs Reservation, as it was then called, was redesignated Platt National Park in 1906 by a joint session of Congress. Platt National Park was named to commemorate Orville H. Platt, a United States senator from Connecticut who had been a long-term member of the Committee on Indian Affairs. In 1907 the Oklahoma Territory and the Indian Territory in which the park was located were joined and admitted to the Union as the state of Oklahoma.

The park rapidly became a popular health spa, and by 1930 Sulphur, which had come to be called the "Summer Capital," had developed into a major resort city of more than four thousand permanent residents. The city and park became favorite vacation and convention spots for

Oklahoma and much of the Middle West. A large hotel, several bathhouses, swimming pools, and other tourist facilities were built in Sulphur to serve visitors to the park. The mineral waters from the park's springs were in such demand that they were commercially bottled and distributed. The belief in the therapeutic value of the bromide water was so popular during one period before World War I that the park superintendent limited visitors to a single gallon of Bromide Spring's limited output.

In the early years of the park's existence there was very little development of the facilities one sees today. With the exception of the popular area around the mineral springs, much of the park remained unfenced and unkempt for many years because of meager funds made available by Congress. Not until the early 1920's was cattle grazing and limited farming on the park's upland formally and permanently forbidden and the areas restored to native vegetation. In 1933, however, a Civilian Conservation Corps camp was established in the park, and the greatest development in the park's history began. Indeed, the park one sees today is largely the product of the labor of those young men in the years between 1933 and the camp's deactivation in 1940. Most of the roads, foot trails, picnic areas, and rock work were completed during those years. Perhaps most significant were the landscaping efforts undertaken by the C.C.C. One such project was the beautification of the boggy areas around Antelope and Buffalo springs. The large muddy area was filled and graded to facilitate local drainage. Then Buffalo Springs was dug out and lined with native stone to produce the clear, bubbling pool so many visitors have come to enjoy. Another beautification and conservation project which is appreciated today more than ever before was the setting out of 800,000 plants of all types throughout the park, including nearly 60 tree species native to Oklahoma.

More recent improvements to the park have been the upgrading of physical facilities such as campgrounds and picnic areas. In 1969 the Travertine Nature Center was completed, and the eastern end of the park was cleared of a portion of the Perimeter Drive and some picnic areas to form the Environmental Study Area. Traces of those facilities can still be seen at several places, but they are gradually being reclaimed by natural vegetation. Coincident with the establishment of the Nature Center was the marking of several self-guiding nature trails.

Future plans call for minor expansion of the park's local boundaries and possible formal consolidation with the Arbuckle Recreation Area to form a single, integrated recreational and interpretive retreat for the growing population of the Southwest.

APPRECIATION OF THE LANDSCAPE

The occurrence of various contrasting landscapes in Platt National Park is one of the most significant aspects of the park. It is one thing to drive into a pleasant natural setting and enjoy a day of casual sight-seeing, swimming, or hiking; it is quite another to have an understanding of how and why those surroundings exist as they do. The goals of any visitor to this park or any other area of natural interest should therefore be twofold.

First, the visitor should develop an ability to observe

what is around him. Too often when visiting the country-side, and especially the national parks and monuments, one expects and usually finds that the more spectacular and publicized sights will indeed demand the visitor's attention and confound him with beauty, size, or some other notable quality. Subtlety, patience, and quietude are therefore qualities not often exercised by most visitors. In Platt, however, breathtaking vistas and dramatic phenomena have in their stead quiet, pleasant vignettes of nature's ageless ways which can only be appreciated through the cultivation of these qualities of mind and methods of observation.

The second goal is that of understanding what one observes. The understanding and appreciation of why: Why are certain slopes grass-covered while others are cloaked with trees? Why does the cactus grow so abundantly atop certain hills? Why are bluffs formed along certain stream banks? These aspects of natural growth can only be understood through patient observation; but understanding, in turn, makes observation much more clear and enjoyable. Thus the two go hand in hand for the enlightened visitor.

Landscapes and Environments

The scenery which one looks upon in the countryside may have various terms applied to it, either in whole or in part. A term which will be used frequently in this booklet, and which is commonly used in geography and geology, is *landscape.* Used in an unspecialized sense, a landscape is simply the sum of all phenomena within a given area, say within the view of the observer. Thus when one speaks of the park's landscape, one is referring to the totality of his visual experience: to all plants, animals, landforms, water forms, human activities, and anything else that exists on that portion of the earth's surface.

Since landscape is such a general and sometimes unwieldy concept, it is often subdivided into units which identify specific environmental processes or agents for easier discussion. One of these units is the *physical landscape,* which includes climate, landforms, water bodies, underlying rock materials of the earth's crust, and the various soils formed upon the surface. The many forms of plant and animal life of an area make up the *biological landscape.* It includes all living things that inhabit the earth, from the smallest micro-organisms in the air, soil, and water to the largest plants and animals. A third aspect of the over-all landscape is sometimes called the *cultural landscape,* and includes those activities and effects which can be directly attributed to man's presence on the earth's surface. Within the cultural landscape of Platt National Park the many roads, trails, buildings, and mowed areas are obvious modifications of the physical and biological landscape's constituent parts. Another term which is sometimes used in place of landscape, but which retains the same general meaning and division, is *environment.* Regardless which term one uses, however, the subject is still the totality of interrelated phenomena which lend character to the face of Platt National Park, and indeed to the entire earth.

2

EVOLUTION OF THE PARK'S PHYSICAL LANDSCAPE

The oldest facet of the environment of Platt National Park, and that which logically forms the foundation for everything that follows, is the physical landscape. It is the inanimate, but certainly not unchanging, stage for all biological and cultural activities. Included in its evolution is the early shaping of the earth's gross features of major geologic proportions, the development of local surface features and their attendant soils, and the origin and character of the various water forms which have helped shape the park.

ANCIENT SHAPING OF THE PLATT-ARBUCKLE AREA

The Precambrian

The sequence of events which has resulted in the Platt-Arbuckle landscape began some twelve to thirteen hundred million years ago during the period of geologic time called the Precambrian era. Very little is known

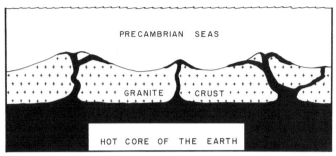

Figure 5. Formation of the earth's crust. The pressure in the earth's hot core forced molten rock, or magma, to the surface. Deep flows of magma cooled slowly to form granite.

about the geologic activity of that period, but it is certain that very large areas of today's continental land masses had not yet emerged from the vast prehistoric seas which covered even more of the earth's surface than the 77 per cent covered today. The only life forms that may have existed were the most simple of marine organisms, such as single-celled algae. Beneath the almost lifeless seas, however, a great deal of geologic activity was taking place. The hot core of the earth was forcing molten rock to flow from many fissures and rifts in the ocean floor. As the countless cubic miles of molten material flowed across the sea floor, it solidified into stable granite rock and formed the crustlike foundation upon which the continent now rests.

The sequence of geologic evolution during the Precambrian period is sketchy, but it is likely that relatively little earth-building activity occurred for some five hundred million years after the continental foundation was formed. During those millions of years the changes in the terrestrial surface nevertheless continued, but at a slower pace. The erosive power of the sea relentlessly wore down the submarine irregularities which had been formed by earlier volcanic activity. Rock particles removed from the "uplands" were eventually deposited across the sea floor to form a rather uniform surface. This material, called *sediment,* was primarily sandy in nature and was approximately a mile thick over the Platt area and increased to as much as three miles in thickness a short distance south. As these deposits increased in depth, the great weight of the overbearing sediments and water caused the sand to become compacted and "cemented" into sandstone through a process called *lithification.* Eventually the sheer weight of the sandstone deposits began to deform the earth's crust, and a significant sag or downward warp began to appear under the thick sediments south of Platt.

The Cambrian
At the onset of the Cambrian period, approximately five

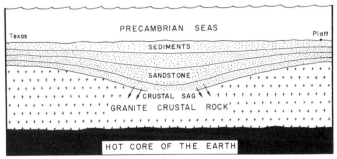

Figure 6.   Early sedimentation and subsidence.

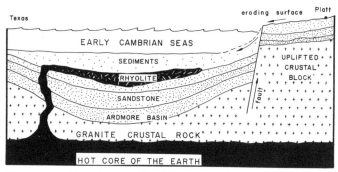

Figure 7. Faulting in the Platt area thrust a portion of land upward above the surface of the sea.

hundred million years ago, the relatively static condition of the crustal foundation in southern Oklahoma was violently ended. Massive upheavals began to occur in the basal rocks, and the crustal sag south of Platt intensified. The degree of sag increased greatly for millions of years, while yet another of these upheavals to the north of Platt began to lift the Platt area sharply. The result of these opposing forces was a huge *fault,* or fracture, in the earth's crust. The Platt area was atop a massive block of the earth's crust, several hundred square miles in area, which was thrust upward far above the surface of the prehistoric sea. The sandstone cap of this elevated block, which had been part of the sea-floor sediment, was subject to all the erosive agents of the sea, atmosphere, and gravity. The sand and sandstone fragments which eroded from the uplifted Platt block also made their way into the southern down-warp, which began to take on the characteristics of a major geologic basin. This basin extended from the Platt area to near the present-day border of Texas and in modern geologic terminology has come to be known as the Ardmore Basin. During the following one hundred million years the Ardmore Basin became still more pronounced as it filled with new igneous material, which flowed from hot magma chambers deep within the earth. This was rhyolite, a heavy granitelike rock, whose weight placed still greater stress on the warped granite crust and overlying sandstone sedimentary rock.

The Ordovician

Although the massive flows of Cambrian rhyolite did not intrude into the Platt area, later developments radically changed the local geology. The Ordovician period of the Paleozoic era saw the continued existence of a broad sea which covered much of the United States. An area from Texas to Wisconsin and from Missouri westward to Colorado was inundated, including the eroded fault block area of Platt that had earlier been lifted above sea level. For the next two hundred million years marine sediments again accumulated to great depths over the

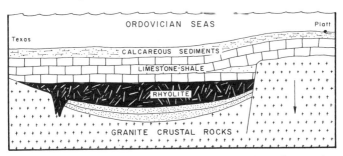

Figure 8. Inundation of the Platt National Park area by an Ordovician sea.

sea floor. These sediments were much different from the earlier sands. By that time marine life had made vast developments, and mollusks, fishes, invertebrates, and a host of other organisms were abundant. The bodies of these organisms were rich in calcium, and as countless generations of them died, their remains settled to the sea floor in thick, limy blankets. As time passed, lithification occurred as the mixture of organic debris and nonorganic sediments became cemented together by chemical action and pressure to form limestone. Intermixed with the layers of organic sediments were many layers of predominantly fine clays and silts deposited by sea currents. They were subjected to similar metamorphic activity and evolved into shale, the fine-grained rock one sees in thin layers in the face of Bromide Hill. By the end of the Devonian period, some three hundred million years ago, the granite crust of the earth under Platt was being depressed by deposits of limestone and shale two miles thick.

The Permian
The final and most important episode in the structural formation of Platt took place between 250 and 300 million years ago. During that period both the southern edge of the Ardmore Basin and the Platt fault block were again forced upward in a sudden movement of the earth's crust. Because the upward forces were so great, the layers of sandstone, shale, limestone, and rhyolite that filled the basin were squeezed, broken, and folded in accordion fashion. The largest of the upward convex folds, called an *anticline,* was thrust some seven thousand feet above the sea immediately south of the Platt area and formed the Arbuckle Mountains. During those

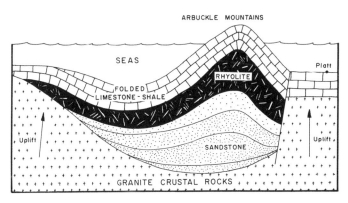

Figure 9. Anticlinal formation of the Arbuckle Mountains which occurred some 250 to 300 million years ago.

millions of years, and continuing through the Permian period, much of Oklahoma and Texas, including the Ardmore Basin and the Platt area north of the Arbuckle Mountains, remained covered by what are called Permian seas. Another deep layer of sediments was deposited on the sea floor during the Permian, but they were mostly bright-red sandstone and shales. These Permian "redbeds" form the bright-red soils one sees today while traveling through central Oklahoma. With the exception of minor local buckling and faulting, the massive earth movement which formed the Arbuckle Mountains was the last to affect the region. Subsequent changes in the geology of the area were largely the result of near-surface activity, such as erosive degradation and sedimentary aggradation, as the Permian seas retreated to the present Gulf of Mexico.

After being thrust so high into the elements, the Arbuckle Mountains, like mountains everywhere, began

An exposure of strata of the Vanoss formation near Rock Creek Campground. Note the dip of the strata to the south (right) and the different rates of erosion. Sandstone and conglomerate both form angular, blocky outcrops, while the shale is sloped and marked by rill erosion. The outcrop near the top is conglomerate, the two outcrops below it are sandstone.

the slow but inevitable cycle of erosion which will someday return them to sea level. The agents of land-form erosion are the elements of weather, such as heat, ice, rainfall, and wind, which mechanically attack the rock structure. There is also a subtle chemical action which causes many of the minerals that bind rocks to-gether to deteriorate. Lastly there is the action of gravity in causing all of the decomposed or fragmented rock to be carried to a lower level, grain by grain, chip by chip. In the Arbuckles much of the erosional debris was car-ried by rain waters down the northern slopes of the mountains. There, logically, the heavier rock fragments came to rest first, followed by increasingly smaller par-ticles the farther the debris flowed.

Today's Surface Geology
The surface rocks seen in Platt National Park today are remnants of the Arbuckle erosion. The surface rock which extends across the park and the surrounding local area is known as the Vanoss formation. Included in it are shales, sandstones, and conglomerates that formed in successive horizontal layers, or *strata,* depending upon the periodically changing rates of erosion through some two hundred million years.

The foot trail which winds up the northern face of Bromide Hill is an excellent place to see all these strata and to traverse some two hundred million years of sedi-mentary deposition. Near the bottom of the hill are some alternating strata of fine-grained sandstones and shales which can be easily broken off or scratched with another rock or a hard stick. Farther up the slope and capping the hill is a very thick layer of conglomerate. It looks like very coarse concrete and contains sands,

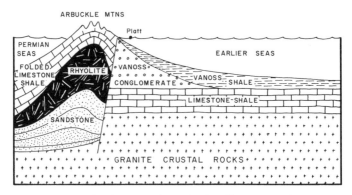

Figure 10. The last two hundred million years has seen periodically changing rates of erosion shape the Arbuckle Mountains.

gravels, and cobbles of various size, all cemented together by natural processes. It is a resistant rock that forms many ridges and outcrops in the Platt-Arbuckle area. The large size of many of the constituent materials in the conglomerate indicates that when that particular stratum was laid down the source of the rock was either very near the park site or else the transporting force was very strong.

DEVELOPMENT OF SURFACE FEATURES AND SOILS

The process which shaped the earth's crust and created the major geologic features of the Oklahoma landscape slowed down some 250 million years ago, but change is ceaseless. If there are any laws or regularities which the earth adheres to as it journeys through space and time,

Thinly bedded strata of shale, sandstone, and conglomerate of the Vanoss formation on the northern face of Bromide Hill. The angularly fractured rock on which this visitor's hand is resting, and that at his hip level, is sandstone; shale is sandwiched between the sandstone and appears again at knee level. The conglomerate which caps the hill begins just above the man's head. Photo by Chester Weems.

one of those laws is the inevitable and unending change which affects all things, not the least of which are the physical features of the earth's crust. The processes which act upon the surface landscape are called *gradational processes,* because they mechanically shape, or grade, major geological structures into the landforms one sees today. The over-all process of change is termed *geomorphism,* and has five geomorphic agents which do the shaping work: streams, underground water, waves and currents, glaciers, and wind. Of these five agents, streams have played the most significant role in shaping the post-Permian landscape of the area around Platt National Park.

The Formation of Rock Creek
Although there is no beginning or end to a landscape, it is likely that the present surface features of the local area, including the park and the city of Sulphur, are the result of the last few thousand years of the Quaternary geologic period. Until that time a stratum of conglomerate rock one hundred or more feet thick capped the series of sandstones and shales which were earlier described in Bromide Hill. The area was originally higher than much of the surrounding terrain by virtue of being close to the Arbuckle Mountain remnants. Additionally, conglomerate is a rock very resistant to nature's erosive forces, and it was more slowly worn down than the rocks of some nearby areas. Nevertheless, the rains which fell during those thousands of years could not soak into the rock but had to find or make a pathway which would eventually lead to sea level. The persistent runoff from a large area north and east of the park site formed a stream which meandered across the conglomerate land-

scape, continually seeking a lower level. For some unknown reason, perhaps because of a fault or a weak area
in the conglomerate, the stream made a niche which it
continued to expand. That stream is today called Rock
Creek, and its niche is now a substantial valley which
extends for many miles and is over 150 feet deep. Much
of Rock Creek's valley has a fairly common appearance,
but there are some landforms which catch one's attention and require an explanation. Bromide Hill is the
most notable example, but the reasons for its formation
can be applied to many similar hills or bluffs in the
vicinity.

When the major earth movements stopped in the
Permian period, the large area of conglomerate and its
underlying strata of sedimentary rocks were not left in
a level position but were slightly tilted in a south-
southwesterly direction. It appears that the high ground
around Sulphur was the northernmost extension of the
conglomerate cap. From the city northward for some
distance the Vanoss formation shale was exposed to the
surface. This set the stage for a process known as *differential erosion,* which is responsible for a great portion
of the earth's landforms.

Differential erosion occurs where two or more earth
materials of different resistance to erosion are in con-
tact. The Vanoss conglomerate is more resistant to
erosion than underlying strata for a number of reasons.
Most importantly, it is an extremely porous rock which
catches rainfall and lets it permeate downward through
the rock rather than forcing the full volume of precipitation to flow across its surface and cause mechanical
erosion. The conglomerate is also made up of relatively
hard rocks which are often larger than baseballs and are

tightly cemented together. As a result, it is very difficult for wind and water to break down and transport the rock materials. On the other hand, the sandstones and shales are made up of sand and fine, silt-sized particles which were formed by only light cementation and pressure compaction and were thus vulnerable to quick destruction. The shale which predominates is also a very compact, nearly impervious material which does not readily pass water. When water falls upon the shale formation or flows across it in a stream, virtually all of it races across the surface and creates a drainage system of rills, gulleys, and eventually large valleys. The fine grains of the rock surface are then easily dislodged and carried away by the running water.

The Carving of Bromide Hill

As Rock Creek sought the easiest path to sea level, it established its course across the landscape very near the northern edge of the conglomerate cap. Through the years its ceaseless erosive action began to erode vertically and create a V-shaped valley, and the stream channel also started lateral erosion. Such lateral erosion of stream banks is normal, but in this case it progressed in one predominant direction—the south—and into the present park area. The reason for this southward migration of the channel is the force of gravity "pulling" the water downward along the easily eroded slope, or dipping plane, of the shale strata. Thus Rock Creek is incising the Bromide Hill mass much as a road grader cuts at the side of a large earth bank along a country roadway. The result of this migration is a typical asymmetrical valley with a shallow gradient on the north next to Sulphur and an abrupt rise, known as a *bluff,* on the

A large block of conglomerate which long ago tumbled into Rock Creek after being undercut by the stream.

southern bank of the stream. The most obvious example of the undercutting action of Rock Creek is near Bromide Spring.

As such undercutting proceeds, the overhanging rock will eventually become too heavy for existing support, and it will break off and tumble into the stream channel. Room-sized remnants of one such rockfall are visible in the creek about one hundred yards east of the entrance to Rock Creek campground. Along other parts of the hill the undercutting is less spectacular because gravity works through *mass wasting* to continuously transport smaller portions of rock and soil down the face of the hill, where they are removed by the streams and deposited elsewhere. If this erosive action of Rock Creek continues without a major disruption, Bromide Hill will someday be totally removed.

Travertine Creek

The eastern end of the park encloses the valley of Travertine Creek. It is a more common symmetrical valley which for many thousands of years was shaped solely by periodic, or *ephemeral,* runoff, which resulted from local rain storms. The unusual point of this valley is not easily recognized by eye although it is discernible from maps, aerial photographs, or detailed walks through the area. This point of interest is the sudden broadening and flattening of the valley floor which occurs west of Buffalo and Antelope springs. The springs, of course, are responsible for the sudden increase in size because of their equally sudden appearance and erosive capability. East of the springs the valley remains V-shaped because it is still a channel for only storm drainage, and even some of that is trapped behind the dams of ranch ponds outside the park's boundaries.

Soil Development

Another facet of the park's landscape is the mantle of soils and alluvium, or *regolith,* which blanket the geologic landforms. The development of this soil blanket is significantly affected by all the factors of environment: vegetation; the landform where the soil is forming; the rock, or "parent material," which furnishes the raw materials; the climatic conditions; and the period of time over which these factors work. Once a visitor is aware of these soil-forming factors and their effects on

An exposure of the deep, dark alluvial soil typical of the park's lowland. Its high clay content allows it to tolerate such vertical cuts. Note the surface litter and tree roots which add organic matter to the soil. Photo by Chester Weems.

the regolith, soils become one of the clearest indications of changing environment. As one walks through or visits different areas of the park, one should match the soil to his other surroundings.

The lowland areas of the park along the streams have developed the deepest soils and those which one would normally think of as fertile and valuable for agriculture. They are generally clay loams that are generally seven to ten feet deep. For the most part these soils were formed of sediments which were moved from one area to another by stream action. Such parent materials are called *alluvium,* and they can be either rich in nutrients, which is the case in the park, or they can be generally "worthless," as they are along sandy streams. Since most of the lowland alluvium was carried from the exposed shale strata north of the park, the soils tend to be rich in silt, clay, and organic matter. These soils are also like the parent shale in that they absorb a great deal of water but hold it in the soil structure instead of allowing it to drain through, as do sandy soils. Although new by the scales of geologic time, these are fairly old and stable soils in human years. Consequently, they have also had the opportunity to develop specific site characteristics.

In general one can expect the deepest, darkest soils on the flat lowland. There may be some sand mixed into the upper few inches from periodic flooding, but it will become a heavy reddish-brown clay a few inches or so beneath the surface. Because the lowland soils are under a moderately heavy growth of vegetation they are shaded and tend to remain moist during all seasons. The forest floor *litter,* which is composed of decaying foliage and wood, produces mild organic acids which permeate the upper *horizon,* or layer, of the soil and

A natural levee which was deposited by flood waters in 1970 can be seen in the right foreground of this photograph of Rock Creek's bank.

characterizes nearly all forest soils. Many kinds of plant roots penetrate these soils to several inches or feet and some of the larger lowland trees, such as sycamore, will have roots extending to several yards in depth. This soil is also rich in micro-flora and fauna.

Within a few tens of yards of Rock Creek's channel one can often find a great deal of light-colored sand either in the channel or atop the banks. This sand came primarily from the decomposition of local sandstones and is too heavy to be carried very far by normal or flood-stage stream water. Whenever there is high water, it therefore comes to rest near the stream bank, while finer and lighter silts are carried away. Such ridgelike sand accumulations, whether obvious or indistinct, are known as *natural levees.* The last such deposits in Platt National Park are the result of serious flooding in the autumn of 1970.

The farther one proceeds from a stream bottom, the shallower and drier the soils will become. In the first place, it is harder for the streams to make distant deposits of alluvium; second, the soils which do form on the site are subject to greater erosion because of the increasing slope. Soils which form in place from weathered parent material are often created no faster than they are carried downslope, and so they maintain a relatively constant depth which decreases with the steepness of slope. Slopes also encourage drainage, which consequently reduces soil moisture.

An interesting exception to this general rule is found along the foot trail up the face of Bromide Hill. On some of those fifty-degree slopes the shale strata have weathered into fairly deep soils. These soils constantly slip and wash down the slope, but the dense vegetation cover and its network of roots protect and anchor the soil to an amazing degree. This slope also stays unusually moist because it is shaded and sheltered from the afternoon sun and prevailing summer winds.

The soils of the park's uplands are universally formed from the coarse Vanoss conglomerate. None of these soils have been deposited by water but have formed where they are as *residual soils.* Most of the upland soils on all sides of the park are therefore very shallow soils of gray-brown color that are mixed with a great deal of gravel and cobble. The general term applied to this category of soil is "rough-stony." Because the conglomerate

Dark soil, several inches in depth, is retained on the steep and wooded slopes of Bromide Hill by a dense network of tree and grass roots shown above the pick handle.

weathers into soil-sized particles so slowly, these soils are commonly only two to eight inches deep. Even that depth is largely filled with rocks, and without a substantial cover of grass or shrubs these soils either blow or wash away as quickly as they form. As circumstance would have it, the rapid drainage and the upland exposure of the conglomerate make it frequently too dry for such vegetative protection. This combination of soil-forming factors results in the alkali or base rich soils which characterize semi-arid grasslands.

Between these two markedly different soils there is a

This roadcut along the Perimeter Drive exposes part of the conglomerate stratum and shows the formation of a thin and stony layer of soil. Photo by Chester Weems.

transitional spectrum which can best be observed along one of the foot trails that traverse the valley side. Perhaps the best trail for such a study begins just east of the Travertine Nature Center on the south side of Travertine Creek.

THE PARK'S WATERS

The waters of Platt National Park have always been of interest to the visitor not only because of their refreshing qualities but also because of the mystery which springs have always held for many people. It is hoped that the facts of their origin and characteristics will be equally interesting.

At least thirty springs of both fresh and mineral water are found within the park's boundaries. There are also several more "seeps" where water oozes from the rock or soil, several of which can be seen along various foot trails. Most of the springs are found in one of two areas. The fresh-water springs are centered in the extreme east end of the park, and the mineral springs are clustered around Bromide Hill. Some of the springs produce impressive quantities of water, but none approach the size of many in Arkansas and Missouri, which produce tens of millions of gallons a day.

The origins and nature of the park's springs are classic textbook models. Virtually all the soils and rocks which mantle the earth's crust contain varying amounts of moisture known as *ground water*. The ability of any portion of these upper layers of the earth to contain ground water, and the amount they hold, depends on a few elementary physical conditions. First, since all ground water was originally precipitation, the greater the rainfall in a given area the greater the potential ground water source. Likewise, the more porous the soil or rock the greater its capacity for storing or transporting ground water, much like a sponge or a wick. Lastly, the force of gravity moves the water from one point to another.

As we have said, Platt National Park is situated in an area of ancient sedimentary rocks which were tilted and folded several hundred million years ago. The high ground in the park is capped with a permeable limestone conglomerate, but under the conglomerate are

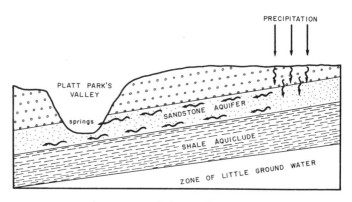

Figure 11. The origin of the park's springs.

alternating strata of shale and sandstone, which are the rock elements essential to the existence of Platt's springs. The park is situated on the lower northern slope of one of the massive rock down-folds, or *synclines,* which was formed in the Permian period. Since that time erosional processes have degraded and truncated the syncline to expose a broad cross-section of the various strata a few miles east and south of the park.

The vertical sequence of the exposed strata happens to be favorable for the formation of springs because the permeable conglomerate and the porous sandstone are closest to the surface, where they can absorb and transport a maximum of the precipitation or surface water they receive. Such conductive rock and soil strata are known as *aquifers.* Directly under the sandstone is a massive layer of impermeable shale which acts as an *aquiclude* and blocks further vertical infiltration of the ground water. Without this impervious stratum the water might pass into deeper strata and be unavailable as a spring source. Gravity forces the ground water vertically downward until it reaches the shale aquiclude. From there the water moves down the dip or slope of the shale until it finds a surface exit or moves into the deeper rock past the park.

In Platt National Park some of the water was provided with a surface exit by the action of surface erosion. Rock Creek and the ephemeral waters that flowed over the eastern end of the park area carved their channels progressively deeper into the sandwiched Vanoss formation until both streams cut into the water-filled sandstone strata. The resulting springs now add their waters to both channels.

Fresh-Water Springs

Antelope and Buffalo springs are the largest of the springs in the park. They and the other fresh-water springs have their origin in a catchment area several miles east of the park and flow through sandstone of the Pontotoc group. Since water from these springs has no distinctive odor or taste, it is called "fresh" water, but in fact it contains a great deal of calcium carbonate in solution. The Pontotoc sandstone is apparently high in calcareous content, and this is dissolved as the water infiltrates toward the park. It is this heavy load of calcium carbonate which precipitates to form the travertine rock, or calcareous tufa, mentioned in Chapter 1. Because of the depth of the water-bearing sandstone beneath the surface and the many years the water rests in the rock, the springs have a year-round water temperature of sixty-six degrees.

The major fresh-water springs have either run dry or been severely curtailed in flow several times in the last century, and always after a long drought. Once rains come again, the aquifer is recharged, and the volume returns to normal. A more serious threat to the springs recently has been heavy water-well pumping in the area east of the park. The wells remove water from the sand-stone aquifer faster than it is replenished by rainfall. It may be a matter of only a few years before man disrupts the springs and, in turn, the ecology of this valley and others like it elsewhere.

Mineral Springs

All the park's mineral springs have a great number of compounds in solution, but it is the bromine and hydro-gen sulphide compounds which are so predominant that they lend their names to most springs. The water for these springs comes from a catchment area approxi-mately two hundred feet higher, twelve miles southeast of the park. It is an area of exposed sandstone of the Simpson group. This particular sandstone stratum formed adjacent to a stratum of oil-bearing sands in ancient geologic times. When the Permian folding took place, the two beds were squeezed together and com-pressed so that the petroleum was forced into the porous spaces of the Simpson sandstone to form natural as-phalt. Until a few years ago that asphalt was commer-cially mined, and some of the abandoned workings are still visible west of Arbuckle Dam. It is from the petro-leum compounds in the Simpson sandstone that the slowly permeating water absorbs its many minerals. Mineral waters are not commercially pumped around Platt National Park, and, although some of the mineral waters flow intermittently, park officials say that there is no foreseeable danger to their continued existence.

3

ECOLOGY OF THE PARK'S BIOLOGICAL LANDSCAPES

Thus far in this book attention has been centered on the physical factors of the park as they act in apparent independence of other aspects of the environment. That is of course not the case but is only a convenient method of approaching one aspect of our subject at a time. In this section the focus will be on the relationships among the living things which occupy the park area—the biological landscape—and some of its ties to the whole environment. Such a study is what is known as *ecology*.

Perhaps one way of viewing the full extent of ecology, and of understanding the functions of the broad categories of the environment, is to draw an analogy with a theater. The stage and sets of the natural theater are the hills, valleys, waters, and winds of the physical landscape. All are constantly changing but give the transient and relatively short-lived human being an impression of submissiveness to the whims of more animate creatures. The actors in this theater can be represented by the flora and fauna, which exhibit the most marked changes in personality and role from season to season and year to year. Profoundly affecting both theater and actors is mankind—an actor himself—with his directorlike energies who, for a few centuries now has had a significant impact on the progression of the drama. Like the theater reviewer, who must consider all aspects of a production but devotes most of this attention to the performance of the actors, the ecologist deals with all the factors of a landscape but primarily focuses on the relationships between the plants and animals of an area.

ECOSYSTEMS

Throughout this book we have consciously used the terms *flora* and *fauna* to describe the components of the biological landscape. Seldom does one refer to the *individual* plant or animal which is a genetically uniform entity, or even to a local *population* of a certain species of organism. The reason for this is that isolated individuals or separate populations do not exist in spatial or physiological isolation. Rather, all living organisms depend upon some other living organism for some part or task in its life-support cycle. Although one looks upon an apparently independent and solitary geranium in a window flower pot and may see no other living thing, there are in fact many dozens or even hundreds of different organisms at work to keep that plant producing those cheerful red blossoms. The soil alone contains many micro-organisms which are invisible to the human eye but which are nevertheless as important to the life of the geranium as the periodic watering and cultivation by the gardener. Indeed, the interdependent relation-

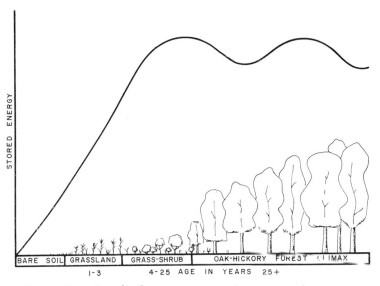

Figure 12. Graph of energy storage in a vegetation succession. When energy input approximates energy output, a climax condition has been reached.

ships among *all* living things In a portion of the earth's surface are so complex that they are dealt with as a system—an *ecosystem*.

An ecosystem may range in size from a small, living-room terrarium to thousands of square miles of tropical rain forest. The most important characteristic which all have in common, however, is their ordered and effective system of physical and biological interrelationships. What must be kept in mind is that such a system of ordered relationships is not a fixed entity in which there is a standard composition of citizens. Ecosystems are what are called "open systems," which constantly change in their dimensions and constituent members. These changes are the result of arrivals and departures of various environmental factors across the indefinite boundaries of the ecosystem—thus the use of the word "open."

All ecosystems undergo evolutionary change, but the logical and theoretical goal of all these changes is an improved ecosystem which approaches a stable and balanced state of existence known as a *climax* community. Such a community exists when the energy and material arrivals in an ecosystem exactly balance the sum of the departing energy and mass (assuming in this atomic-nuclear age that mass and energy are not simply different forms of the same phenomenon). Although scientists disagree on the exact state of a climax community—or indeed on the philosophical question whether change ever stops—for all practical purposes the climax community is the optimum association of living things for a given set of physical conditions. It exists when the rate of change in the system becomes imperceptible to historic observation.

The process of reaching the climax stage is known as *succession* because individuals, populations, and associations of conditions succeed one another in waves or cycles of always diminishing energy fluctuation. An obvious example of succession is regularly opposed each year by farmers and gardeners. Assume for a moment the case of a flower bed located in a lush, green lawn of Bermuda grass. The grass of the lawn stays attractive and vigorous because all the environmental conditions favor its growth over other plants in the immediate area. The portion of the yard which is devoted to the flower bed shares the optimum growing conditions with the lawn, except that it is subjected to regular and intense periods of environmental disruption in the form of the gardener's weeding and cultivation. If perchance the gardener becomes involved in other activities which detract from his attentions, the disruptive spells of gardening become less intense and frequent, and the Bermuda grass wastes no time sending out "runners," or rhizomes, to claim the territory. First, however, will come a crop of small and large mixed annual weeds, such as dandelions or crabgrass, to try its hand as a successional stage. It may dominate for a short period but will soon share the soil's surface with the increasing mat of Bermuda rhizomes. A few days later the Bermuda cover will be complete, and the local ecosystem will be essentially stable until some major environmental change is induced by man or nature.

Within Platt National Park is an excellent example of a successional process in the Environmental Study Area east of the Nature Center. Until 1969 the Perimeter Drive extended through that portion of the park and was paved with asphalt. When the Environmental Study Area was established, the asphalt was removed, and the area was allowed to revert to natural vegetation. Grasses and annual herbs that thrive in open sunlight and with scant competition from fellow plants were the first to establish themselves. After the grasses had established some sod and contributed to the organic content and moisture-holding capacity of the soil, shrubs and juniper from the surrounding forest margins began to encroach. As these shrubs and small trees grow, they shade the sun-loving grasses which forged their first home and cause the grasses and herbs to diminish. In coming years the increase in shade and soil moisture will provide an acceptable site for the germination and growth of the large

An example of succession along an abandoned roadway in the Environmental Study Area.

broadleaf trees of the oak-hickory forest. Two or three decades from now the oak-hickory community will complete the cycle to a local climax by shading out all the original shrubs and creating conditions favorable to the growth of a greenbrier, wild-grape, and redbud understory.

Plant communities and stages of succession within those communities have distinctive vertical structures which usually appear as strata in the foliage. In plant studies there are eight recognized and potentially present strata: (1) moss or lichen, (2) annual herb, (3) perennial herb, (4) low shrub, (5) tall shrub, (6) seedling tree, (7) understory tree, and (8) overstory tree.

Vegetation undergoes the most obvious changes in a successional process, but it is not the only changing aspect of the ecosystem. Because of the myriad interrelationships which exist among all parts of an ecosystem, a change in one necessitates some degree of adaptation in nearly all elements, both physical and biological. Of most interest to man are the subsequent adjustments in soil character, micro-climate, and fauna. These adjustments are often so subtle and coordinated that it is difficult to ascertain which are causal factors and which are effects.

Land which has been cleared of its native climax vegetation (be it grass, shrub, or forest) by some traumatic means such as fire, cultivation, or persistent overgrazing, is immediately exposed to the full effects of the sun, wind, and rain. These are disruptive and destructive to normal soil development. The most pronounced effect is often loss of soil moisture through wind and sun evaporation followed by erosion of better developed upper horizons during strong winds and rains. Less fertile lower horizons which are thus exposed to the surface can seldom support the kind or density of vegetation that was originally present. Decreased moisture also makes the ground unsuitable for germination of many seeds or as a habitat for burrowing soil creatures that do nature's "cultivation."

In the case of the abandoned roadway, grasses were soon established, and they provided some protection from the weather. The grasses formed a root network which helped keep the soil loose, inhibited erosion, added organic matter, and held soil moisture. As larger herbs, shrubs, and juniper become established, their litter and shade will increase soil moisture and acidity,

Winter scene on Travertine Creek. Photo by Chester Weems.

and conditions for forest plants will improve as soil conditions change.

The changes in vegetation largely induce the local expansion or shrinkage of animal habitats. The lizards, flies, and butterflies which frequent sunny areas, as well as other small herbivores—such as rabbits, mice, and birds which feed on the grasses and forbs—retreat to other domains as the forest encroaches on the old roadway. They are replaced by animals such as the salamander, the mosquito, and the oppossum, which find the shadows and moisture suitable. All the while the greatest formal migration of all has gone on totally unnoticed by size-centric human beings. It is the concurrent ebb and flow of thousands of species of insects, bacteria, fungi, mosses, and other organisms which make the ecosystem work.

FOOD CHAINS

Of all the interrelationships which tie an ecosystem together, perhaps none is so basic or important as the *food chain*. An understanding of the principles and workings of the food chain is therefore essential to the understanding of an ecosystem or landscape. The stages of energy use in the food chain are called *trophic levels*, levels of nourishment and processes of taking and utilizing food. It is, like the ecosystem as a whole, also an open system which can be considered a cycle for practical purposes. In that cycle the basic life-forming and energy-producing earth elements, such as calcium, phosphorus, iron, carbon, and oxygen, are repeatedly reused by one or more species of living things.

An arbitrary but convenient starting point for a discussion of the food chain and its various trophic levels is the soil. Soil is the home and site of much organic activity in its own right, but perhaps most important is its role as the storehouse of the minerals of which all living things are composed. A similar role is played by the sun, the ultimate source of all nonnuclear energy on this planet. The natural elements and minerals in the soil were once physically bound up in the crystalline structure of the rocks which form the earth's crust, but

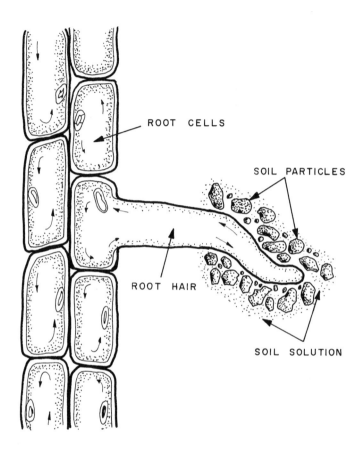

ROOT CELLS

SOIL PARTICLES

ROOT HAIR

SOIL SOLUTION

*Figure 13. A root hair magnified to show its relation-
ship with the soil particles and soil solution from which
the root obtains essential elements for growth and repro-
duction. From Donahue et al., 1971.*

through chemical and mechanical weathering they have been released for use in the surface landscape. Once near the surface, the weathered or decomposed rock mixes with living and dead organic matter to form soil. All that is needed to release the soil's minerals for use by living organisms is water to dissolve and transport the minerals to the roots of plants. At that point the nutrients first enter the life stream and begin their journey upward through successive trophic levels, or stages in the food chain.

Trophic level one is the most critical, although all have an important role in any ecosystem; its primary function is the generation of food material and oxygen, and its members are known as *producers*. Producers are green plants and algae which in the presence of sunlight perform photosynthesis. This is a complex reaction whereby carbon dioxide gas, taken in by the leaves from the atmosphere, and water, taken in by the roots from the soil, are converted into free oxygen gas, and a carbohydrate by certain tissues in the plants. Carbohydrates are a form of food which the plant stores in its roots, leaves, or other tissues. The carbohydrates remain in storage until needed to sustain the plant, until the plant dies, or until the plant is eaten by another organism and the stored energy is released through metabolic processes. At the same time the plant is manufacturing and storing energy in the form of carbohydrates, its own body structure is formed from the minerals of the soil. These minerals are food not in the sense that they produce energy but insofar as they are in turn digested and assimilated into the structure of the organism consuming the plant.

The successive blocks of trophic levels in the food

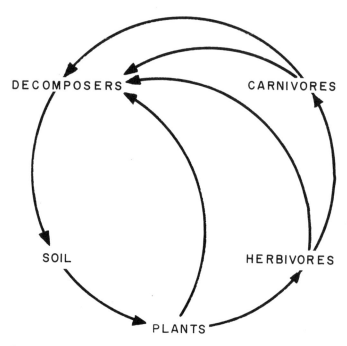

Figure 14. A simplified model of the food chain.

chain are representative of *consumers*. These are organisms which actively consume other organisms to sustain themselves. Included in the consumer group are trophic levels two, three, and even four. Trophic level two is composed of those animals which eat the producing plants. Consumers at this level are called *herbivores* because they eat nothing but plants, common examples being grasshoppers, sparrows, rodents, and cattle. Trophic levels three and four are represented by consumers which are still further removed from the source of plant energy. They are secondary consumers because they live exclusively by eating herbivores or primary consumers. Consumers such as eagles or frogs which eat only flesh are known as *carnivores,* while some—like human beings, bears, and raccoons—transcend all consumer levels by eating both meat and vegetable matter. Members of the latter group are known as *omnivores.*

The fifth and last trophic level of the food chain is made up of all the small organisms which live upon *dead* organisms, either plant or animal. These organisms— bacteria, fungi, and protozoa—which cause things to "rot," are called *decomposers.* The decomposers are universally small creatures which immediately attack and devour any dead creature to secure food. The waste products from their activities are the various gases and waste material which give dead and decaying material a distinctive odor. In fact, decay is the physical mani- festation of these decomposing organisms at work. What material they do not use in their own life-support cycles is released to the soil or atmosphere in the form of basic elements and minerals, which are soon recycled through the plants of the first trophic level. At that point the food chain is said to be complete

4

LANDSCAPES AND ECOSYSTEMS OF THE PARK

One of the major points of interest in Platt National Park is the existence of an *ecotone*, or boundary between two major kinds of ecosystems. This ecotone is unique in that it is not a broad transition but occurs very abruptly within the limited confines of the park. Because of the abrupt and abbreviated nature of this change, it is obvious to anyone who is expecting it and is an excellent example to study and use as a teaching illustration.

The two major ecosystems which meet each other in the park are the eastern deciduous forest and the western short-grass, or steppe-type, prairie. Each of these ecosystems has a core area in which it is most intense in its manifestation. That intensity declines as the distance from each core increases, and between the typical deciduous forest and the short-grass prairie one finds a transitional landscape which has some characteristics of each of its neighboring ecosystems. Neither of these ecosystems, occurring in close proximity in the park, qualify as theoretical or even regional cores representing their communities, but they suffice on a local basis. At this point it is important to note that ecosystems are often named after their dominant forms of vegetation, but this is only a matter of convenience and in no way excludes from the discussion the full range of flora and fauna.

THE LOWLAND LANDSCAPE

The dominant ecosystem in the lowlands of the park is one of the westernmost extensions of its kind in Oklahoma. It is a southwestern remnant of a huge prehistoric forest which once covered much of the earth's northern hemisphere. Repeated glaciations of the Pleistocene, or "ice age," and increased human settlement in historic times destroyed most of the forest, and the best and richest example long remained that of eastern North America. The forest was once contiguous and of relatively homogeneous composition, but thousands of years of climatic change and plant migration have resulted in regional differences. The southern forest is generally recognized as an oak-hickory community.

A Natural Mature Community

The best example of a mature deciduous forest ecosystem in the park is the dense woodland along Travertine Creek in the Environmental Study Area. There one can see a local climax condition of the eastern deciduous forest. The conditions necessary for this ecosystem are localized in the valley bottom, and so most of this forest is concentrated within several hundred feet of the stream. This is the narrow band of deep alluvial soils which have

The dense and multilayered vegetation of a climax lowland forest near Travertine Creek.

great water-holding capacity and low drainage gradients. These soil conditions in conjunction with acceptable climatic conditions happen to provide an environment in which the oak-hickory community thrives and outpaces all other ecosystems.

As one strolls along one of the bottomland trails of the Environmental Study Area, the stratification of the forest becomes obvious once the visitor is aware of the characteristics. Most of the dominant trees, which form an *overstory* some seventy-five to one hundred feet above the ground, are spotted (Texas) oak and bitternut hickory. Both trees have spreading crown tops which reach out for the intense sunlight these trees need. The trunks of both may be as large as two or three feet in diameter. The oak is covered with a dark, ridged, thick bark, while the hickory trunk is protected by a medium-gray, fairly smooth bark. The sycamore is also prevalent where water is abundant, for example, very close to the stream. It is one of the largest trees in size and bulk in a temperate forest. It has a large spreading crown, a trunk perhaps four feet in diameter and a distinctive bark. Most of the bark is light gray and very smooth because it is constantly flaking off. Only very old trees or lower trunks have a thick, dark, furrowed bark.

The next stratum one sees below the dominant overstory trees is the large group of shade tolerant trees of the *understory*. These trees not only tolerate but prefer less sunlight, lower temperatures, and higher humidity, found in a zone twenty to fifty feet above the ground. The southern hackberry, roughleaf dogwood, and redbud are typical of this group. All these trees have slender trunks and crowns that tend to flatten and spread out to catch all possible sunlight filtering through the overstory.

The shrub stratum includes those plants whose fully mature height is between about two to twenty feet and many tree seedlings whose mature size is much taller. This layer varies a great deal in density and frequency of species from area to area. Commonly seen at this level are the red mulberry, Mexican plum, winged elm, American elm, and dogwood.

The strata lower than shrubs are largely vacant in this portion of Platt because ground litter is so thick and shading so nearly complete that it is difficult for grasses and mosses to grow. That is not to say that this level of the ecosystem has no members nor that all parts of this forest area are without substantial numbers of these plants. It simply means that they do not form a prominent part of the community viewed by man.

As one views the forest, it becomes obvious that not all plants grow in a series of clearly defined upward steps or that all trees of a stratum are of the same height and lushness of growth. One may find immature trees and shrubs progressing through any intermediate level on their way to their "place in the sun." Other plants which transcend the formal strata are climbing vines, such as wild grape. Many of these vines, some as large as one's arm and extending well up into the understory, can be seen along the various trails. There are also other plants, such as the parasite mistletoe which, although less than a yard in diameter, may live at any level on a host tree.

Lowland Forest Variations
The lowland forest have noticeable variations in composition even within a small area like the park. Three of these variations merit mention. The first occurs throughout the park to some degree, but is most marked along

Artificially thinned and cleaned woodland around Rock Creek.

the course of Rock Creek. Along the fringes of this stream in the old sand deposits and flood-washed banks that receive more sunlight and water, one finds a lower stratum of annual and perennial herbs, as well as two additional trees. Here the cottonwood and various species of willow thrive on banks and occasional sandbar islands. The cottonwood is a massive, quick-growing tree of the poplar family, which is the sole marker of many intermittent stream channels in arid country. Despite its size, the cottonwood is easily damaged and short-lived, and its thick-barked, craggy trunk provides homes for many kinds of wildlife. The willow is usually a brushy tree with

The immature woodland in Rock Creek Campground shows small trees reaching for sunlight under intense competition.

many suckerlike growths that form a dense barrier on stream banks. Because of its density, tenacity, and ease of planting, it is an excellent erosion-control agent.

The valley bottom between the park's main entrance and Rock Creek campground is a man-induced variation of the climax lowland forest. In this part of the park there has been no effort to maintain a natural forest, but rather to create a pleasant parklike atmosphere. An overstory of oak and elm still predominates, but the expected lower strata have largely been eliminated by years of mowing and human activity. Many members of the natural community have been eliminated, and in their place we see imported species which are more compatible with heavy use. Under these conditions the only way this portion of woodland can be perpetuated is through human effort, such as transplantation and protection of seedlings.

The last variation of the lowland forest is the wooded area of Rock Creek campground. Here one sees a community which is constantly struggling to reach the stability of a climax stage. That climax has probably been repeatedly delayed in the past by local flooding, grazing of livestock, or human activity. As a result there is a dense growth of immature overstory and understory tree species, few of which have become dominant enough to shade out lower strata plants that probably could not survive in a climax forest.

Animals of the Lowland Landscape

Thus far in the discussion of the lowland landscape we have been concerned only with the plant life, but it comprises only part of the living ecosystem, even though it is the most obvious and accessible portion of the biological landscape. It forms a large part of the all-important framework, or matrix, within which the various species of animals gather food, find shelter, and raise their young.

The stream banks and immediately adjacent moist areas in the valley are the habitat of several species of amphibians. Most commonly seen is the small leopard frog, which leaps into the stream with a squeak as strangers approach. It feeds on insects near the surface of the streams, and is itself prize fare for several other woodland animals. The frogs, toads, and salamanders of this environment generally live in holes in the muddy banks.

There are many reptiles throughout the lowland, but no poisonous snakes have been seen in the park for several years. Probably they were driven away by the large number of visitors. There are large numbers of rattlesnakes and some cottonmouth snakes in the surrounding area, however, Near the streams are many water snakes, such as diamondback and blotched water snakes. Garter and ribbon snakes also frequent the moist areas. All of these are harmless and feed largely on insects, salamanders, and small frogs. The prairie kingsnake and the black rat snake inhabit the drier lowland and transitional slopes. Both eat large numbers of rodents and other small animals, and the kingsnake has a special appetite for other snakes and lizards. Both of these snakes prowl at night and spend daylight hours in almost any sheltered spot, such as under logs and rocks. Turtles are common in the eastern end of the park, especially the three-toed box turtle and the ornate box turtle. Both of these reptiles are dry-land creatures which will eat almost anything but subsist mostly on grass and leaves. Their hiding places are scratched-out depressions in the soil and ground litter. Bleached shells of the turtles are frequently found on the forest floor.

The mammals in the lowlands of Platt National Park are representative of those found in any eastern lowland forest—with one exception. The exception is the armadillo, which is found largely in Gulf Coast regions and an area through the southern Plains states and whose range is rapidly expanding. This armored animal is a little larger than a house cat and usually lives in a burrow in a ravine or hillside. It feeds largely on insects and grubs, which it roots out of the forest-floor litter. It is very common in the park and is occasionally seen, but is more often de-

Figure 15. The raccoon is primarily a nocturnal animal found near streams.

tected by the narrow winding furrows it makes each night in the forest litter in search of food.

The opossum and the raccoon are common nocturnal forest dwellers whose presence in the park can most readily be detected by their sign. Both feed along stream bottoms where they live mainly on large insects, bird eggs, small mammals, and, in the case of the raccoon, marine animals like frogs, crayfish, and turtles. Their footprints are easily seen along stream banks and on soft soil. The opossum also makes distinctive scratches in the bark of trees while climbing to rest or in search of bird nests to rob.

Squirrels and skunks are also prevalent in the park, including the southern flying squirrel. A small group of these squirrels can be seen near the Travertine Nature Center, leaping and gliding between trees during quiet periods of the morning and evening. They build exterior nests of leaves and twigs or adopt abandoned woodpecker holes. Their feed varies with the season but normally includes nuts, seeds, fruit, and some insects.

The most profuse and varied animal life in the lowlands is the bird community. Approximately 150 different species of birds have been seen in or flying over the park, and most of them either live in or temporarily visit the lowland forest environs. More than those of any other animal, the number and composition of the bird population vary seasonally. The complexity of the vegetative community is responsible for the variety in bird life found in the park. It is dense and varied and has multiple strata, which present a great range of habitats. The park is also a protected enclave, where each bird species can sustain itself with minimal disruption.

Each of the bird species has a separate niche which it

occupies in the ecosystem. It prefers a certain kind and age of tree for nesting, roosting, and feeding. It also has a preferred stratum in the forest, as well as a bounded area it claims as its own domain. In return for these privileges the bird must contribute to the plant community. He does so by eating insects which attack trees, by pollinating many types of plants, and by carrying the seeds that ensure new generations of habitat-producing plants.

In the lower and understory trees of the forest visitors will frequently see the easily recognized blue jay and the eastern cardinal. Both can be seen sitting on lower branches or dropping to the ground for food. The blue jay is omnivorous and eats berries, seeds, and forest-floor insects, as well as scraps of food left by park visitors. It is very common around the campgrounds in the western end of the park. The cardinal prefers seeds and a little less human company, but it is very common, especially in the eastern half of the park.

The eastern bluebird is a common lowland resident which catches both ground and flying insects for its primary diet and eats wild berries during winter months when insects are in decline. That is just one example of the seasonal adjustment of an ecosystem's food chain. Woodpeckers also control insect pests, particularly those inaccessible to most other birds. It has been estimated that in a well-balanced forest ecosystem woodpeckers find and eat over 90 per cent of the bark-dwelling insects and grubs. Several species, such as the common red-headed and the western red-bellied woodpeckers, can be seen and heard at all times of the day.

An infrequent but easily seen and identified resident of the Rock Creek area is the belted kingfisher. This large, crested, blue-gray bird sits perched on tree branches several feet over the stream, and when it spots a small fish, it dives head first into the stream and emerges with dinner in its beak. It is probably the only fishing bird regularly found in the park. One of the greatest fish eaters, the bald eagle, is rare in this region and has not been seen in the park, though it is sighted occasionally near Lake of the Arbuckles. There are several predators in the park. One of the most conspicuous in the lowland is the northern barred owl. It is a large bird, nearly eighteen inches long. It sits in stream-bottom trees during all times of the day and is not easily disturbed by human activity. It feeds on small mammals, birds, and insects which it swoops down upon. It performs the same role in the thick forest as hawks do in more open terrain.

Last there is the carrion-eating turkey vulture, which one can see on nearly any day gliding over the forest or open country searching for a dead animal. Its keen eyesight finds carrion and soon brings others to share it. It serves the very useful purpose of breaking down and largely removing the carcasses of larger animals. In their absence it would take weeks for insects and decomposing organisms to remove dead animals and return their nutrients to the soil. In this way the vulture is a link in the circular food chain of the ecosystem it inhabits.

All these representative animals, and hundreds of others that could be listed (see Appendix 1), are integral members of the lowland ecosystem and depend to some degree on each other. No less than the birds, all other living things have distinct niches which they must fill— no single member is the keystone of the structure whose presence or absence is paramount—all living organisms share that honor and responsibility.

An area of dense short grass covering the conglomerate upland west of Rock Creek. Trees in the background are on stream valley slopes.

THE UPLAND LANDSCAPE

The upland of Platt National Park, with its slopes and conglomerate-capped hills, forms a totally different physical environment from that of the stream valley, slightly over one hundred feet below. Much of the change is the result of *physiographic aridity,* a dry environment which is caused by landform factors, such as the steep slopes and extremely permeable conglomerate which mark Platt's uplands. Because it is a different physical environment from the lowlands, there has evolved a different

*Bunch-type short grass on very thin and dry upland soil.
Photo by Chester Weems.*

biological environment suitable to the droughty conditions.

Short-Grass Prairie

The most widespread ecosystem of the upland is the
short-grass prairie, which has a natural range in dry areas
from mid-Oklahoma westward to the High-Plains fringe
of the Rocky Mountains in Colorado, and from central
Canada southward into Mexico. This community thrives
on ten to thirty inches of precipitation a year and with-
stands both droughts and temperature extremes. In areas
of relatively high moisture the short grasses form a fairly

This upland grass land behind Bromide Hill has been invaded by woody shrubs, yucca, prickly pear, and many juniper trees.

Prickly-pear cactus. Photo by Chester Weems

dense and uniform soil cover, but on the dry fringes or locally dry areas hardier bunch grasses and other *xerophytic,* or dryland, plants predominate.

Nearly all of the upland along the park's southern boundary is in grassland, but the area atop Bromide Hill between Rock Creek campground and the western Bison Viewpoint is the most accessible. That area would probably have been considered a local climax short grass community when the site became a park. At that time the only vegetation over its greatest extent was a single stratum of herbs. Most of the surface was covered with blue grama, hairy grama, or the hardy buffalograss. Patches of soil which were too dry to support those solid-cover grasses yielded to bunch grasses of the bluestem family, such as little sand and silver bluestem.

Yucca. Photo by Chester Weems.

In addition to grasses, the droughty areas of upland soils have supported members of the cactus family and other xerophytes which can survive the harshest local droughts and even expand their range as grasses thin and decline. Foremost in this category is the prickly-pear cactus. This sprawling cactus, with its fleshy and thorn-studded pads and seasonal fruits, is notorious throughout the west for invading pastureland. Ranchers blame the prickly pear for ruining range land, but in truth the cactus can only survive and spread on land where it has little competition. This situation is found on range land which has been abused by man or otherwise ruined for optimal grazing, usually because of poor range management. Occurring along with the prickly pear in Platt National Park is the small echinocereus cactus, a plant two to four inches tall with a rounded, kegshaped body. It is found growing only on the stony soils of the highest and driest portions of the park. More common is the yucca, which is widespread in the clearings of the uplands. It is a plant that reaches a height of one to two feet, with narrow thorn-tipped leaves and an inverted cone-shaped profile.

Grassland Succession

In the years since the park was established, this apparent climax vegetative scheme has been modified, seemingly through well-intentioned human interference. Parts of the grassland now have substantial areas covered with a shrub stratum and some trees of almost understory dimensions. Encroaching shrub growth is largely seedling oak, chickasaw plum, and sumac. The oak grows singly and slowly, but the plum and sumac quickly form dense thickets on sunny slopes and eventually dominate and shade out the original grasses.

The most conspicuous tree on the upland grassland is the red cedar, or juniper. This tenacious tree will grow nearly anywhere and has apparently found the conglomerate uplands very much to its liking since it was introduced to the park during the 1930's. It spreads across suitable land very quickly because its pea-sized berries are a favorite food for some birds, and the seeds pass through the digestive system unharmed. Another rapidly spreading tree is the brushy persimmon, which seems to have an affinity for abandoned fields and fence rows. It is often found with the small Chickasaw plum tree, and both can be seen covering much of the overgrazed pasture land outside the park's southern boundary. During the spring and early summer months the scrubby plum trees are covered with small but delicious fruit.

The causes of the increase in tree and shrub cover on previous grassland are possibly the same factors which have caused former treeless prairie in other regions of the United States to become wooded in recent decades. Man has overgrazed this grassland to the point where some trees and shrubs are able to gain a foothold in the patches of bare soil in what was once a solid sod cover. Others thrive, as they do in the park, because fences and surrounding human habitation reduce or eliminate browsing, grazing, and trampling by both wild and domestic herbivores. Buffalo, antelope, deer, and cattle will serve such a role if they are allowed to frequent an area. Last, the region is protected from range fires which once claimed much of the prairie each year. Grasses were able to seasonally rejuvenate from seed and sod, but the slower-growing woody plants were eliminated by burning. As a result of those changes in the total environment, there has been an inevitable change in the tenant ecosystem, in this case to a mixed range of grass and shrub.

Animals of the Upland Community

The upland environment is more harsh and restrictive than that of the lowland, resulting in a smaller variety of plant life. Consequently it is the habitat for fewer species of animal life, although still more than the park visitor might expect.

There are two common reptiles in the upland ecosystem of the park. The easiest to see is the six-lined racerunner lizard, which one can frequently spot darting across trails and roads. This lizard, six to nine inches long, feeds on insects and lives in holes or small burrows under rocks and litter on dry upland soils. More difficult to see is the Texas horned lizard, commonly called the horny toad. This broad, flat, sandy-colored lizard will remain nearly motionless for hours while catching ants and other insects near the ground. It likewise uses a convenient depression or hole under vegetation or rocks for its resting place.

The mammals that inhabit the upland are nocturnal creatures, and it is seldom that a visitor will see them unless he is equipped with patience and a good flashlight. The largest mammal population anywhere in the park is probably that of the upland-dwelling white-footed mouse. Each acre of grass and brush is the home of several dozen of the small, seed-eating creatures. Their nests are tiny burrows under rocks or tufts of bunch grass, and the trails where they run at night in search of food appear as a network of furrows through the grass. Another prominent member of the upland margins is the eastern wood rat, sometimes called the pack rat. This rodent is about the size of a house rat. It makes its large outdoor nest under a tree or in a bush or thicket. It builds its nest into a dome-shaped pile of sticks, leaves, and other forest-floor debris. One can see such nests along several of the upland trails in the eastern end of the park. This rat also is a herbivore, living primarily on seeds, nuts, and the wild fruit that he can forage within a short distance of his nest.

Another nocturnal visitor in and near the park's uplands is the coyote, the most common and widespread wild member of the canine family in North America. This animal digs its den or takes over another animal's abandoned burrow on high and relatively open ground. There are probably no dens inside the park, but the animals frequent the uplands in search of food, such as mice and rats. The coyote is therefore a member of the third or fourth trophic level and serves to control the numbers of rodents in its home range. The coyote has no enemy except man's often ill-conceived and unjustified extermination campaigns. Many campers would feel a serious spiritual loss if the coyote's yipping and howling were no longer heard in the night.

Birds, having the greatest mobility of all the animals, visit upland grass and scrub growth in great variety and abundance, depending upon the season and time of day. Those most readily seen there, however, are the birds which depend most directly on those areas for food. Several members of the sparrow family, especially the western field sparrow, are predominant. These small birds usually nest in low trees in or near the grassland and live on the seeds of grasses and other low plants. The cedar waxwing changes locality frequently, but its craving for small fruits and berries makes it a regular resident of juniper-covered uplands, such as Bromide Hill. There it feeds almost exclusively on the small juniper berries and is largely responsible for increasing the range of the juniper by carrying the seeds over wide areas in its digestive tract.

Within the bird family the hawks fill the same role as that of the coyotes on the ground. They are the hunters or predators which appear over the uplands at various times of the day. One which is very frequently seen sitting on poles or trees in the afternoons is the small sparrow hawk. As sunset approaches, this highly maneuverable bird can be seen darting, swooping, or soaring

Figure 16 (opposite). Example of an upland food chain found in Platt National Park.

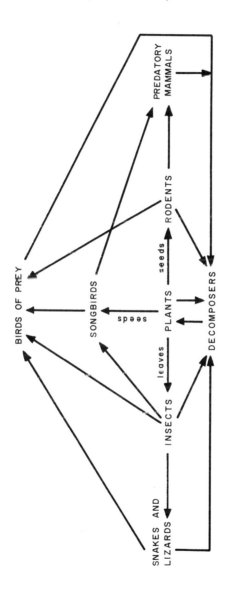

through the air as it catches its principal diet of flying insects. The sharp-shinned hawk can be seen at any time of the day, swooping high and low over the upland margins as it preys on smaller birds. The largest hawk which is common in the park is the red-tailed hawk. This hunter has a wingspread that reaches to as much as four feet and a conspicuously rusty-red tail which makes it one of the easiest hawks to recognize. It nests in the tops of woodland trees but hunts the open grassland, where it can successfully attack animals as large as rabbits. The red-tailed hawk feeds primarily on rodents and is therefore seen late in the afternoon soaring in circles, using its almost uncanny eyesight to spot game that ventures out too early or too boldly.

The animal life which has been discussed here comprises only a small portion of all the moving creatures in the upland ecosystem. They are, however, fairly representative of the types that live there, the ones visitors might catch some sign of, and ones which point out the basic relationships of the upland food chain.

The greatly simplified diagram shown here illustrates these relationships and the flow of energy and nutrients within the food chain. Of course, any number of other relationships and animals could be portrayed. There are likewise changes in every food chain resulting from seasonal or environmental changes which alter food sources and habitats.

TRANSITIONAL LANDSCAPES

It is obvious that not all of the park's area lies within either the lowland-forest ecosystem or the grassy-upland

A small segment of the distinct transitional boundary along the conglomerate upland. Note the beginning of grasses and cactus plants where the scrubby tree growth stops. Photo by Chester Weems.

ecosystem. Narrow as it is, the transitional area, or eco-*tone*, between the two climax types of landscapes has characteristics of its own that will be of interest to the visitor. The location of the transitional ecosystem is largely the area of moderate slopes between the stream valleys and the tops of the conglomerate-capped upland. The most significant determinant of the rate of transition or change of the ecosystem is the increasing physiographic aridity from lowland to upland. The vegetation of this transitional zone consequently represents a spectrum of *mesophytic* plants (those receiving a well-balanced moisture supply) through *xerophytic* (dry land) plants.

The Oak-Elm Transitional Community

In the eastern end of the park the transitional community is an oak forest whose principal members are the
Texas and chinquapin oak. Texas ash, American elm,
and bitternut hickory are important minorities in the
upper stories. The understory on the lower slopes is
largely redbud, winged elm, and red mulberry; but on
upper slopes it is quickly replaced by Mexican plum,
shining sumac, and a multitude of herbs. The forest edge
forms a distinct line along the lower edge of the conglomerate stratum in this area, with only scattered scrub
growth deviating from the natural boundary of the
community.

This particular transition zone is the habitat for at
least three animals which are seldom seen in other areas
of the park. Foremost is the eastern bobwhite quail,
which seems to prefer stream-valley ecotones—shade,
protective cover, and water are provided by wooded
valleys, while the fringing grassland provides the quail
with its diet of seeds and small fruits. Coveys of these
birds are frequently encountered along the easternmost
trails of the Environmental Study Area.

Another visitor or resident of the area is the bobcat, a
nocturnal hunter with a range of several miles. It makes
its den in nearly any dry, protected place away from
human beings and feeds on the small animals of the
forest fringe, such as quail and rodents.

According to tracks and other signs the white-tailed
deer also makes occasional forays into the east end of
the park to drink from the streams or to browse on the
leaves and stems of shrubby vegetation. The white-tailed
deer is the largest animal that is still running free in the
park environment.

The Post Oak Community
The upland slopes in the west-central portion of the park have a vegetation community which is overwhelmingly dominated by the post oak, but nonetheless contains substantial numbers of Texas ash and winged elm. The post oak is a bushy tree of medium size which forms a dense cover over poor upland soils in much of eastern Oklahoma and Texas. It is commonly twenty to forty feet tall in the park and has a trunk diameter of several inches. At one time it was widely used for fence posts and construction timber, hence its name. The understory associated with the post-oak forest is largely seedling or stunted versions of the upperstory, as well as many shrubs, such as Mexican plum and sumac. Native grasses struggle for survival amid the leaf litter of open spaces.

The Short-lobed Oak Community
A last variation in the transition zone is found on the northern rim and face of Bromide Hill, where a community of short-lobed oak mixed with some post oak and Texas ash has formed an almost impenetrable thicket. For some reason the short-lobed oak found this dry outcrop, with all its exposure to the weather elements, to be a very suitable area for growth. It forms the most homogeneous community in the park and is not evident in significant numbers elsewhere. Within that small forest the short-lobed oaks, from ten to fifteen feet in height, dominate in all strata. Only infrequently does the scrub stage of another tree emerge from the forest floor, which is uncharacteristically deep in leaf litter. Junipers and squawbush sumacs flourish in the sunlit fringes of the narrow band of trees.

5
MAN'S IMPACT ON THE PARK'S LANDSCAPE

Of all the creatures which have walked the earth in the hundreds of millions of years since life began, none have had so profound an impact on the environment as *Homo sapiens*. All other creatures have fulfilled their natural roles in their respective ecosystems, struggling for survival, propagating their species, and returning their bodies to the soil in an unconscious recycling process. During those millions of years of life on earth a great many changes, whether imperceptible or catastrophic, have occurred. Unknown thousands of plant and animal species have come and gone, and the earth's surface itself has been reshaped by the natural elements. It is significant to note, however, that all these changes were either evolutionary or only locally traumatic. They were the result of natural and inevitable laws or regularities that seemed to guide or shape the biological and physical landscapes.

It was only when man appeared—with his unexceptional body but extraordinary capacity for rational action—that landscape changes of "extra-natural" proportions began to occur. As we all know, man has not been satisfied to fill a natural niche in his ecosystem in the same manner as a chimpanzee or an orangutan. We have been able to reason and imagine what our lot could be like with certain changes. First we modified our ecosystems by selectively killing or domesticating certain plants and animals, and by modifying our habitat. Now we manufacture our ecosystems to a large degree or assemble them from a myriad of desirable components we have imported to our sites. Great amounts of energy and nutrients are transported around the globe to meet local desires, and, in the end, when man's short life is gone, the egocentricity of our species largely requires entombed burial. Not even our bodies return to nourish the earth and complete the cycle.

It is not likely that man's nature will change. Indeed, it is argued by some philosophers that man, as a rational citizen of the earth, is as much a part of the "natural" landscape, and his actions a part of natural evolution, as a toad, a sparrow, or any other nonthinking creature. It is possible, however, to change man's role and to increase his awareness of his own impact on the environment. We see Platt National Park as a site for illustrating a few instances of the actual or potential impact of human activity. Most of these instances are obvious, but people simply do not think about them very often.

How many of us have been irritated at home or work by the tiresome or raucous noise of construction machinery, truck traffic, or a motorcycle, especially when we are trying to sleep or relax? Probably a great many people would admit to that. Why, then, should we not be concerned when trail bikes not only disturb our en-

Not-so-silent spring. The noise of machines disturbs the quality of a natural environment.

joyment of the outdoors but cause still greater damage to the habitat of local wildlife. Many bird and animal species are not as tolerant to environmental disruption as man, and increased noise levels drive them away or alter their reproductive habits. Is there no refuge from machinery and electronics in the remnants of natural America?

In 1916 and again in the autumn of 1970 the park's valley was ravaged by floodwaters that rose as much as twenty feet above the stream banks after a few hours of rainfall in the local drainage basin. On both occasions there was extensive damage to the park's facilities, ani-

Damage to the park's landscape is still widely evident two years after a flood (photographed 1972).

mal habitats, plant communities, and aesthetic attractions. To many persons this was another natural occurrence brought about by heavy rains. Rains were certainly major factors in both cases, but even more important may have been the accumulated effects of human tampering. The drainage basin around the park has in the past one hundred years largely been cleared of its native vegetation as land has been either cultivated or placed in pasture. Clearing of native vegetation inevitably lessens protection from weather elements, allows the soil to become compacted, and destroys organic matter. Once these things occur, the erosional resistance and water-holding capacity of the soil are markedly reduced. Rather than a time-delayed watershed by infil-

Note the contrast between the frequently overgrazed pasture in the foreground and the natural landscape inside the park's boundary fence in the background.

tration, the result is a basin of sheeting surface runoff. Not only does eroded upland material silt up lower streams and obstruct drainage but heavy rains result in heavy and rapid runoff and lowland flooding.

A problem closely related to many of the effects mentioned above is overgrazing of land which is naturally suited for pasture. Native grasses without irrigation simply cannot reconstitute themselves rapidly enough when grazed excessively. Bare patches of soil that are vulnerable to wind erosion soon appear. These dry patches are then invaded by economically worthless xerophytic growth, such as prickly pear, yucca, and juniper, and the loss to the rancher and the grassland ecosystem begins to intensify. The difference between a frequently overgrazed pasture and protected upland grass can be seen in many places astride the park's southern boundary fence.

One widespread and harmful attitude in the United States is at last being publicly attacked as erroneous. It is the obsession for eliminating all forms of predatory wildlife in the interest of game management or agricultural economics. Predators such as foxes, coyotes, wolves, bobcats, cougars, hawks, and eagles have an essential role to play in any ecosystem where they can survive naturally. Most accounts of damage to livestock by these animals are either erroneous or exaggerated. Their toll of game animals and birds is their natural right, and is more than compensated for by their destruction of "economically harmful" creatures such as rodents. These hunters and predators are some of this country's most beautiful and valuable wildlife.

There is likewise no constructive reason for eliminating any species of plant or animal. Somehow the extinction or local destruction of a species leaves man and the world a little poorer—a little more estranged from nature. In the practical sense, there is the possibility of serious damage to the food chain of the inclusive ecosystem. It does little good to protect birds of prey, for example, if we conduct an organized campaign to trap and poison undesirable rodents. Without rodents in the food chain many hunting birds and mammals would soon starve and diminish in numbers. Without rodent competition and losses to predators, small birds might multiply to levels that would be both bothersome to man and harmful to bird populations. The point to remember then is that destruction of one species causes a ripple of disruption throughout the entire ecosystem.

The addition of new organisms to an ecosystem can also disrupt it to some extent. Some of these measures are intentional ones to make an area more attractive or useful to man. Platt National Park has dozens of plants which were introduced by people in recent years. Most of these plants are trees, flowers, or ornamental shrubs which were introduced on a small scale and have been adopted into the park's biological community without noticeable ill effect. The Bermuda grass which blankets many of the lowland picnic and pavilion areas, the Johnson grass along roads, and the upland juniper are all introduced species.

One of the harmful additions to the wildlife of the park and surrounding countryside is common to many rural areas near towns. The population of feral cats and dogs, neglected or abandoned by their owners, revert to instinctive means of getting food. Feral cats are especially common in the park's lowlands, where they may take a heavy toll of native wildlife. Many livestock kills attributed to natural predators are often the work of feral dogs which are both knowledgeable of man's habits and unafraid to forage near human habitations or activities.

The important thing to remember from these examples is that all human activity has an effect on our surroundings, just as every stone thrown into a pond makes neverending ripples. In a world that is increasingly pressed for open spaces and natural enclaves, man must start to consider the aesthetic, physical, and biological impact of his actions before he puts them into effect. Perhaps the application of courtesy and the golden rule to our natural environment would be an important first step for all of us.

6
CONCLUSION

We sincerely hope that you have enjoyed this introduction to Platt National Park. Although very small, the park, as you now know, is rich in both natural and cultural history.

Although there are many things to see and do while visiting the park, it is our wish that you and your family will begin to look upon the park with an ecological perspective. The park is much more than a plot of land with interesting vegetation and landforms, and it has a greater function than merely serving as a habitat for unique animal associations. The park as a whole can be considered analogous to a living organism. In such an organism, with all its integral organs functioning to ensure survival, if only one important component is perturbed or destroyed, the entire organism suffers. Similarly, in a complex ecosystem, such as that represented in Platt National Park, if any one element of the system is significantly altered, the entire system may suffer.

It is for this reason that Platt National Park should be

considered a natural ecological laboratory where the interdependency of the system components is maintained for the visitor to observe, the scientist to study, and everyone to appreciate. It is a laboratory where natural and cultural perturbations of the system can be observed and analyzed. From such laboratories will come knowledge that may be required for proper management of ecosystems in a world that is undergoing rapid transition. After all, how are we to know and understand the full impact of man's actions on the environment unless we have these natural areas to use as a standard?

FLORA AND FAUNA OF THE PARK

The following lists represent the various flora and fauna found in Platt National Park. The lists have been given discrete headings ("Grasses," "Trees," "Birds," and so on), and each section has been arranged to present both the common and the scientific names of each species, as well as a column for noting observations.

GRASSES

____Big bluestem   *Andropogon Gerardi*
____Hairy grama   *Bouteloua hirsuta*
____Hairy tall dropseed   *Sporobolus asper* var. *pilosus*
____Hairy triodia   *Tridens pilosus*
____Little bluestem   *Andropogon scoparius*
____Purple Three awn   *Aristida purpurea*
____Rough triodia   *Tridens elongatus*
____Side oats grama   *Bouteloua curtipendula*
____Switch grass   *Panicum virgatum*
____Yellow Indian grass   *Sorghastrum nutans*

TREES/COMMON SPECIES

____Ash, green   *Fraxinus pennsylvanica lanceolata*
____Ash, Texas   *Fraxinus texensis*
____Cedar, red   *Juniperus virginiana*
____Cottonwood, southern   *Populus deltoides*
____Dogwood, roughleaf   *Cornus drummondii*
____Elm, American   *Ulmus americana*
____Elm, slippery   *Ulmus fulva*
____Elm, winged   *Ulmus alata*
____Hackberry, southern   *Celtis laevigata*
____Hickory, bitternut   *Carya cordiformis*
____Oak, burr   *Quercus macrocarpa*
____Oak, chinquapin   *Quercus muehlenbergii*
____Oak, post   *Quercus stellata*
____Oak, spotted, or Texas red   *Quercus schmardii v.
texana*
____Oak, short-lobed   *Quercus breviloba*
____Redbud, Texas   *Cercis reniformis Engelm*

——Sumac, shining   *Rhus copallina*
——Sumac, smooth   *Rhus glabra*
——Sycamore   *Platanus occidentalis*
——Walnut, black   *Juglans nigra*
——Willow, black   *Salix nigra*

TREES/UNCOMMON SPECIES

——Ash, prickly   *Zanthoxylum americanum*
——Ash, red   *Fraxinus pennsylvanica Marsh*
——Ash, white   *Fraxinus americana*
——Bittersweet   *Celastrus scandens*
——Bois d'Arc or Osage Orange   *Toxylon pomiferum*
——Box Elder   *Acer negundo*
——Catalpa, common   *Catalpa bignonioides*
——Cherry, Indian   *Rhamnus caroliniana*
——Cherry, perfumed   *Prunus mahaleb*
——Chinaberry   *Melia azedarach*
——Chittam wood   *Bumelia lanuginosa*
——Dogwood, flowering   *Cornus florida*
——Hackberry, Georgia dwarf   *Celtis pumila georgiana*
——Hackberry, Texas   *Celtis laevigate texana*
——Haw, black   *Viburnum rufidulum*
——Hickory, Arkansas   *Carya buckleyi arkansana*
——Hickory, black   *Carya buckleyi Durand*
——Hoptree   *Ptelea trifoliata*
——Hoptree, softleaf   *Ptelea trifoliata Mollis*
——Locust, black   *Robinia pseudoacacia*
——Locust, honey   *Gliditsia triacanthos*
——Maple, silver   *Acer saccarinum*
——Mulberry, paper   *Broussonetia papyrifera*
——Mulberry, red   *Morus rubra L.*
——Mulberry, white   *Morus alba L.*

___Oak, blackjack   *Quercus marilandica*
___Oak, reddish post   *Quercus stellata rufescens Sarg.*
___Pecan   *Carya pecan*
___Persimmon   *Diosypros virginiana*
___Pine, shortleaf or yellow   *Pinus ecninata*
___Plum, bigtree   *Prunus mexicana*
___Plum, Chickasaw   *Prunus angustifolia*
___Plum, wild   *Prunus americana*
___Plum, wildgoose   *Prunus munsoniana*
___Paloblanco, Netleaf Hackberry   *Celtis reticulata Torr.*
___Poplar, silver   *Populus alta L.*
___Soapberry   *Sapindus drummondii*
___Squawbush   *Rhus trilobata*
___Willow, sandbar   *Salix interior Rowlee*

MAMMALS/COMMON SPECIES

___Armadillo, Nine-banded   *Dasypus novemcinctus*
___Bison   *Bison bison*
___Bobcat   *Lynx rufus*
___Coyote   *Canis latrans*
___Fox, Gray   *Urocyon cinereoargenteus*
___Mole, Eastern   *Scalopus aquaticus*
___Mouse, Deer   *Peromyscus maniculatus*
___Mouse, House   *Mus musculus*
___Mouse, White-footed   *Peromyscus leucopus*
___Muskrat   *Ondatra zibethicus*
___Opossum   *Didelphis marsupialis*
___Rabbit, Eastern Cottontail   *Sylvilagus floridanus*
___Raccoon   *Procyon lotor*
___Rat, eastern wood   *Neotoma floridana*

_____Rat, Hispid Cotton   *Sigmodon, hispidus*
_____Shrew, Short-tailed   *Blarina brevicauda*
_____Skunk, Striped   *Mephitis mephitis*
_____Squirrel, Fox   *Sciurus niger*
_____Squirrel, Southern Flying   *Glaucomys volans*
_____Vole, Woodland   *Microtus pinetorum*

MAMMALS/UNCOMMON SPECIES

_____Bat, Evening   *Nycticeius humeralis*
_____Bat, Eastern Pipistrelle   *Pipistrellis subflavus*
_____Bat, Red   *Lasiurus borealis*
_____Beaver   *Castor canadensis*
_____Deer, White-tailed   *Odocoileus virginianus*
_____Fox, Kit   *Vulpes velox*
_____Fox, Red   *Vulpes fulva*
_____Gopher, Plains Pocket   *Geomys bursarius*
_____Mink   *Mustela vison*
._. Mouse, Brush   *Peromyscus boylii*
_____Mouse, Harvest   *Reithrodontomys fulvescens*
_____Mouse, Northern Grasshopper   *Onychomys leuco-
                                        gaster*
_____Mouse, Plains Harvest   *Reithrodontomys montanus*
_____Rabbit, Black-tailed Jack   *Lepus californicus*
_____Rabbit, Swamp   *Sylvilagus aquaticus*
_____Rat, Norway   *Rattus norvegicus*
_____Shrew, Least   *Cryptotis, parva*
_____Skunk, Spotted   *Spilogale putorius*
_____Squirrel, Gray   *Sciurus carolinensis*
_____Squirrel, Thirteen-lined grnd   *Citellus
                                    tridecemlineatus*
_____Weasel, Long-tailed   *Mustela frenats*

BIRDS/COMMON SPECIES

___Bluebird, Eastern *Sialia sialis*
___Bobwhite, Eastern *Colinus virginianus*
___Cardinal, Eastern *Richmondena cardinalis*
___Cowbird, Brown-headed *Molothrus ater*
___Crow, Common *Corvus brachyrhynchos*
___Cuckoo, Yellow-bellied *Coccyzus americanus*
___Dickcissel *Spiza americana*
___Dove, Western Mourning *Zenaidura macroura*
___Flicker, Red Shafted *Colaptes cafer*
___Flicker, Southern Yellow Shafted *Colaptes auratus*
___Flycatcher, Northern Crested *Myiarchus crinitus*
___Gnatcatcher, Blue-gray *Polioptila caerula*
___Goldfinch, Common *Spinus tristis*
___Hawk, Northern Sparrow *Falco sparverius*
___Hummingbird, Ruby-throated *Archilochus colubris*
___Jay, Northern Blue *Cyanocitta cristata*
___Junco, Pink-sided *Junco mearnsi*
___Junco, Slate-colored *Junco hyemalis*
___Killdeer, Northern *Charadrius vociferous*
___Kingbird, Eastern *Tyrannus tyrannus*
___Kingbird, Western *Tyrannus verticalus*
___Kingfisher, Eastern Belted *Megaceryle alcyon*
___Kinglet, Eastern Golden Crowned *Regulus satrapa*
___Meadowlark, Eastern *Sturnella magna*
___Meadowlark, Western *Sturnella neglecta*
___Mockingbird, Eastern *Mimus polyglottos*
___Nighthawk *Chordeiles minor*
___Nuthatch, White-breasted *Sitta carolinensis*
___Oriole, Baltimore *Icterus galbula*
___Oriole, Orchard *Icturus spurius*
___Owl, Northern Barred *Strix varia*

____Pewee, Wood   *Contopus virens*
____Phoebe, Eastern   *Sayornis phoebe*
____Marten, Purple   *Pronge subis*
____Roadrunner   *Geococcyx californianus*
____Robin, Eastern   *Thurdus migratorius*
____Sparrow, Eastern Lark   *Chondestes grammacus*
____Sparrow, Eastern Vesper   *Pooecetes gramineus*
____Sparrow, Harris'   *Zonotrichia querula*
____Sparrow, House   *Passer domesticus*
____Sparrow, Song   *Melospiza melodia*
____Sparrow, Western Field   *Spizella pusilla*
____Swift, Chimney   *Chaetura pelagica*
____Titmouse, Tufted   *Parus bicolor*
____Thrasher, Brown   *Toxostoma rufum*
____Thrush, Eastern Swainson's   *Hylocichla ustulata*
____Vulture, Black   *Coragyps atratus*
____Vulture, Turkey   *Cathartes aura*
____Waxwing, Cedar   *Bombycilla cedorum*
____Warbler, Eastern Yellow   *Dendroica petechia*
____Warbler, Myrtle   *Dendroica coronata*
____Woodpecker, Red-headed   *Melanerpes erythro-cephlus*
____Woodpecker, Southern Downy   *Dendrocopus pubescens*
____Woodpecker, Southern Hairy   *Dendrocopus villosus*
____Woodpecker, Western Red-bellied   *Centurus carolinus*
____Wren, Carolina   *Parus carolinensis*
____Wren, Texas   *Thryomanes bewickii*

BIRDS/UNCOMMON SPECIES

____Blackbird, Brewer's   *Euphagus cyanocephalus*

____Bluebird, Mountain *Sialia currocoides*
____Bunting, Indigo *Passerina cyanea*
____Bunting, Painted *Passerina ciris*
____Catbird *Dunetella carolinensis*
____Chat, Yellow-breasted *Icteria virens*
____Creeper, Brown *Certhia familiaris*
____Cuckoo, Black-bellied *Coccyzus erythrophthalmus*
____Eagle, Golden *Aquila chrysaetos*
____Falcon, Prairie *Falco mexicanus*
____Finch, Eastern Purple *Carpodacus purpureus*
____Finch, House *Carpodacus mexicanus*
____Flycatcher, Ash-throated *Myiarchus cinerascens*
____Flycatcher, Scissor-tailed *Muscivora forficata*
____Grosbeak, Rose-breasted *Pheucticus ludovicianus*
____Hawk, Eastern Red-tailed *Buteo jamaicensis*
____Kinglet, Eastern Ruby-throated *Reglus calendula*
____Ovenbird *Seurus aurocapillus*
____Owl, Eastern Horned *Bubo virginianus*
____Redwing, Eastern *Agelaius phoeniceus*
____Shrike *Lanius ludovicianus*
____Sparrow, Eastern Chipping *Spizella passerina*
____Sparrow, Gambel's *Zonotrichia leucophrys gambeli*
____Sparrow, Lincoln's *Melospiza lincolnii*
____Sparrow, White-crowned *Zonotrichia leucophrys leucophrys*
____Sparrow, White-throated *Zonotrichia albicollis*
____Starling *Sturnus vulgaris*
____Swallow, Bank *Riparia riparia*
____Swallow, Barn *Hirundo rustica*
____Tanager, Summer *Piranga rubra*
____Vireo, Bell's *Vireo belli*
____Vireo, Blue-headed *Vireo solitarius*

____Vireo, Eastern Warbling   *Vireo gilvus*
____Vireo, Red-eyed   *Vireo olivaceous*
____Warbler, Northern Black-throated Green   *Dendroica virens*
____Warbler, Orange-crowned   *Vermivora celata*
____Wren, Western House   *Troglodytes aedon*

REPTILES

LIZARDS/COMMON SPECIES

____Lizard, Fence   *Sceloporus undulatus*
____Racerunner, Six-lined   *Cnemidophorus sexlineatus*
____Racerunner, Spotted   *Cnemidophorus gularis*
____Skink, Five-lined   *Eumeces fasciatus*
____Skink, Ground   *Lygosoma laterale*

LIZARDS/UNCOMMON SPECIES

____Lizard, Eastern Collared   *Crotaphytus collaris*
____Lizard, Texas Horned   *Phrynosoma undulatus*
____Skink, Broad-headed   *Eumeces laticeps*
____Skink, Great Plains   *Eumeces obsoletus*
____Skink, Southern Prairie   *Eumeces spctentrionalus*

SNAKES/COMMON SPECIES

____Kingsnake, Speckled   *Lampropeltis getulus*
____Snake, Black Rat   *Elaphe obsoleta*
____Snake, Blotched Water   *Natrix erythrogaster*
____Snake, Diamond-backed Water   *Natrix rhombifera*

___Snake, Eastern Hognose   *Heterodon platyrhinos*
___Snake, Prairie Ringneck   *Diadophis punctatus*
___Snake, Western Ribbon   *Thamnophis sauritus*

SNAKES/UNCOMMON SPECIES

___Coachwhip, Eastern   *Masticophis flagellum*
___Kingsnake, Prairie   *Lampropeltis calligaster*
___Racer, Eastern Yellow-bellied   *Coluber constrictor*
___Snake, Plains Blind   *Leptotyphlops dulcis*
___Snake, Red-sided Garter   *Thamnophis sirtalis*
___Snake, Rough Earth   *Haldea striatula*
___Snake, Slender Flat-headed   *Tantilla gracilis*
___Snake, Texas Brown   *Storeria dekayi*
___Snake, Western Milk   *Lampropeltis doliata*
___Snake, Western Rough Green   *Opheodrys aestivus*

TURTLES/COMMON SPECIES

___Turtle, Common Snapping   *Chelydra serpentina*
___Turtle, Ornate Box   *Terrapene ornata*
___Turtle, Red-eared   *Pseudemys scripta*
___Turtle, Three-toed Box   *Terrapene carolina*

TURTLES/UNCOMMON SPECIES

___Slider, Missouri   *Pseudemys floridana*
___Stinkpot   *Sternotherus carinatus*

FISH

___Bass, Largemouth   *Micropterus salmoides*
___Bass, Spotted   *Micropterus punctulatus*

___Bass, White   *Roccus chrysops*
___Bullhead, Black   *Ictalurus melas*
___Carp   *Cyprinus carpie*
___Carpsucker, River   *Carpoides carpie*
___Crappie, White   *Promoxis annularis*
___Dace, Southern Redbelly   *Chrosomus erythrogaster*
___Darter, Orangethroat   *Etheostoma spectabile*
___Gambusia   *Gambusia affinis*
___Killifish, Plains   *Fundulus kansae*
___Minnow, Bullhead   *Pimephales vigilex*
___Shad, Gizzard   *Dorosoma cepedianum*
___Shiner, Bigeye   *Notropis boops*
___Shiner, Blacktail   *Notropis venustus*
___Shiner, Golden   *Notemigonus chrysoleucus*
___Shiner, Plains   *Notropis percobromis*
___Shiner, Red   *Notropis lutrensis*
___Shiner, Sand   *Notropis deliciosus*
___Stoneroller   *Campostoma anomalum*
___Sunfish, Bluegill   *Lepomis macrochirus*
___Sunfish, Green   *Lepomis cyanellus*
___Sunfish, Longear   *Lepomis megalotus*
___Sunfish, Redear   *Lepomis microlophus*
___Sunfish, Warmouth   *Chaenobryttus coronarius*

SUGGESTED READINGS

Carson, Rachel. *Silent Spring.* Boston, Houghton Mifflin Company, 1962.

Dubos, Rene. *So Human an Animal.* New York, Charles Scribner's Sons, 1969.

Ehrlich, Paul. *The Population Bomb.* New York, Ballantine Books, 1968.

Krutch, Joseph Wood. *The Great Chain of Life.* Boston, Houghton Mifflin Company, 1957.

Leopold, Aldo. *A Sand County Almanac.* New York, Ballantine Books, 1970.

Marx, Wesley. *The Frail Ocean.* New York, Ballantine Books, 1970.

Zim, Herbert S. and Paul R. Shaffer. *Rocks and Minerals.* New York, Golden Press, 1957.

REFERENCES

Billings, W. D. *Plants, Man, and the Ecosystem.* 2d ed. Belmont, California, Wadsworth Publishing Company, Inc., 1970.

Brown, Perry E. *"Brief History of Platt National Park."* Unpublished paper, Platt National Park, Oklahoma, 1953.

Burt, William Henry, and Richard Philip Grossenheider. *A Field Guide to the Mammals.* Peterson Field Guide Series. 2d ed. Boston, Houghton Mifflin Company, 1958.

Conant, Roger. *A Field Guide to Reptiles and Amphibians.* Peterson Field Guide Series. Boston, Houghton Mifflin Company, 1958.

Dale, Edward E., Jr. "Preliminary Report on Vegetation and Environment of Platt National Park." Unpublished study, University of Arkansas, 1964.

Donahue, Roy L. *Soils: An Introduction to Soils and Plant Growth.* Englewood Cliffs, New Jersey, Prentice-Hall, Inc., 1971.

Ham, William E. *Regional Geology of the Arbuckle Mountains.* Field Trip Guide Book, Fifty-third Annual Meeting of Petroleum Geologists, 1968.

Morris, John W., and Edwin C. McReynolds. *Historical Atlas of Oklahoma.* Norman, University of Oklahoma Press, 1965.

Odum, Eugene C. *Fundamentals of Ecology.* Philadelphia, W. B. Saunders Company, 1959.

Phillips, George R., *et al. Forest Trees of Oklahoma.* 9th ed. Oklahoma City, Forestry Division, Oklahoma State Board of Agriculture, 1959.

Robbins, Chandler S., *et al. Birds of North America.* New York, Golden Press, 1966.

Sutton, George M. *Birds of Oklahoma.* Norman, University of Oklahoma Press, 1967.

Webb, Robert G. *Reptiles of Oklahoma.* Norman, University of Oklahoma Press, 1970.

INDEX

The paper on which this book was printed bears the watermark of the University of Oklahoma Press and has an effective life of at least three hundred years.

University of Oklahoma Press

Norman